TACKLES
LIKE A FERRET

To John Best wish [signature]

TACKLES
LIKE A FERRET

THE AUTOBIOGRAPHY OF
PAUL PARKER
WITH PAT SYMES

FOREWORD BY SIR ALEX FERGUSON

This edition first published by Pitch Publishing 2013

Pitch Publishing
A2 Yeoman Gate
Yeoman Way
Durrington
BN13 3QZ
www.pitchpublishing.co.uk

A CIP catalogue record is available for this book from the
British Library

ISBN 978-1-90917-843-4

Typesetting and origination by Pitch Publishing.

Printed and bound by CPI Group (UK) Ltd, Croydon, CR0 4YY

Contents

Introduction

PAUL PARKER won 19 England caps and played a crucial part in one of the most famous matches in World Cup history when England lost to Germany on penalties in the semi-final of Italia 90.

Parker was also a key figure in the all-conquering Manchester United sides of the 1990s as Sir Alex Ferguson built his Old Trafford dynasty. Sir Alex acknowledges Parker's contribution to one of the best club sides of the decade.

Parker is still a legendary figure at Queens Park Rangers where he helped take the club to the threshold of the league title and at Fulham where he began his distinguished career.

Chelsea, Derby and Sheffield United were his other league clubs.

Now a commentator on the Premiership from his base in Singapore, Parker has strong opinions on the game and provides a fascinating insight into matches and personalities, past and present.

Foreword by Sir Alex Ferguson

P AUL PARKER is without doubt one of the best signings I have made as Manchester United manager, and was an integral part of the defence I consider to be the best I have ever worked with. The Aberdeen back line that helped me win the European Cup Winners' Cup takes some beating but the quartet of Parker, Steve Bruce, Gary Pallister and Denis Irwin is better even than that great defence.

I look upon Paul's time with us in two ways. I remember what a superb servant he was for our club but there is also a fair element of sadness about his short but great career. He was a really fit, athletic player but he was blighted by one or two injuries that ultimately forced him to retire prematurely.

We first looked at Paul when he was at Fulham as a young centre-half and we had a very keen interest but Queens Park Rangers came in on the blindside and signed him. During his time at Loftus Road, where he formed a successful partnership with Alan McDonald, Paul got a cruciate knee injury in November 1990 that slowed up our decision to go back in for him.

He battled back from that injury and did really well and it was in the summer of 1991, a year after he had helped England to a World Cup semi-final, that we found out he was available. We were in Sweden on a pre-season tour and I heard on the grapevine that Everton had made a bid of

£1.5m. I turned to my chairman Martin Edwards and said this is a player who could replace Steve Bruce, who was beginning to suffer from the wear and tear of playing week-in, week-out and had picked up a few injuries of his own.

I spoke to Paul on the telephone and he confirmed that several clubs including Tottenham Hotspur had started negotiations, so I invited him to Old Trafford to discuss a move. I did what I always do when I am trying to persuade a player to join us and took him to see the stadium in all its glory. That was his mind made up.

As fate would have it, Steve went on to play for us for another five years so we converted Paul into one of the best right-backs in the club's history. I have since seen Sir Bobby Robson describe this diminutive but determined defender as a player who "leaps like a salmon and tackles like a ferret". As always, Bobby is spot on with his description. Paul is a tenacious little player and was the most natural defender we had on our books, which says a lot when you look at the players he lined up alongside.

For a guy who never grew beyond 5ft 7ins he was also tremendous in the air, aided by that fantastic spring that has prompted Robson's unusual comparison. I remember one famous Champions League night against Barcelona in 1994 when I asked Paul to man-mark the great Brazilian striker Romario. Paul did a superb job until midway through the first half when he followed Romario into the middle of the penalty area and Gary Pallister shouted across that he would take care of him. Pally just did not have the pace to keep up with him and Romario slotted the ball past Peter Schmeichel and into the net.

Paul's pace was undoubtedly his biggest strength and on another occasion we were playing our great rivals Liverpool at Anfield in 1993 and leading 2-1 when he was up against Mark Walters on the left wing. One of the Liverpool coaches shouted at Walters to run at Parks. I turned to him and said "glad to see you have done your homework".

I could not believe it and was so stunned that I turned to my then number two Brian Kidd and asked him if I was hearing things. Walters tried to follow his instructions but every time he attempted to beat him on the outside, Paul just stuck out a leg and whipped the ball away.

He was a tremendous competitor and I would have backed him to overcome anyone in a one-on-one situation. He could also fight his corner when he needed to and, if ever subjected to one of Schmeichel's legendary verbal volleys, he was always quick to tell the Great Dane to shut up and get back in his goal.

Paul was of course one of the heroes of the team that ended our 26-year wait for a title in the Premiership's inaugural season, 1992/93, only his second full season at the club. He was also a mainstay of our first league and FA Cup Double-winning side a year later and played superbly in the Cup Final against Chelsea at Wembley.

There are many other great memories from his time with us. No doubt Paul will pick out his well-taken goal against his boyhood heroes Tottenham at Old Trafford in a 4-1 victory in December 1993. Paul played a terrific one-two with Brian McClair and smashed the ball past the Spurs goalkeeper Erik Thorstvedt with all he was worth. His only other senior goal for us was in an FA Cup fourth round win at Reading when he crossed the ball into the top-right corner. Reading's pitch at their old Elm Park home was notoriously bobbly and I think Paul was attempting a clearance when he somehow picked out the back of the net from what seemed like miles out. In the same game Steve Bruce missed an open goal from two yards out and Parks spent the whole journey home taunting him about this.

Off the pitch Paul was adored by everyone who met him and was very popular in the dressing room. He was also the subject of one of the funniest wind-ups I have ever witnessed. Paul has always been addicted to mobile phones, and to this day still has one glued to each ear 24 hours a day. We had just beaten Wimbledon down at Selhurst Park and "Choccy" McClair, the dressing room joker of the time, made sure he beat Paul on to the coach after the game. Choccy was a bit of a whiz-kid when it came to technology and went rifling through Paul's boot bag, found his mobile and managed to change the security code before putting it back in the overhead locker.

When Parks stepped on the bus to begin his mountain of phone calls he was shocked to discover he could not access the handset. He spent the entire four-hour journey back to Manchester slumped in a heap at the back of the coach, sulking because he could not make any calls, until when we got to within six or seven miles of the drop-off point and Brian asked if he could borrow the phone. Paul handed it over but explained he could not get it to switch on. He stared on in disbelief when Choccy not only managed to crack the code but made a call to his wife, saying he would be home in ten minutes. Paul was furious and told Brian he would never speak to him again. It was the funniest thing I have ever seen. The two soon kissed and made up but I don't know if Paul ever got his own back. I doubt it.

Had an ankle injury not intervened, I am certain Paul would have gone on to do what Denis Irwin, another fans' favourite from that era, did and play on for United until he was in his mid-30s.

The injury apart, he was as fit as anyone at the club and played with an energy that many of his contemporaries could not match. It is an energy he still has today and then, like now, he was always buzzing around doing something or other. I still regard the 1994 Double-winning side as the best team I have had during my two decades at United, better even than the side that eclipsed them by winning the Treble five years later.

The 1994 team had the lot. They were physically strong and would fight your granny, had great mental toughness and a wealth of experience. Most of the players were at the perfect age of mid to late 20s and we had young lads like Ryan Giggs, Andrei Kanchelskis – who played in front of Paul – and Lee Sharpe just starting out. There was pace and power throughout the side and Paul more than played his part in what was a very successful unit. Had it not been for the foreign player restrictions that hampered our European exertions, with the likes of Eric Cantona and Schmeichel having to be left out for key games, we would certainly have fared much better in the Champions League.

Needless to say, it was a very tough decision for me to make when the time came to let Paul go, as it was with the whole of that formidable back four. Bruce was the first to depart when he watched from the bench for his final game against Liverpool in the 1996 FA Cup Final and Pallister left to rejoin Middlesbrough two years later. It is always sad when you have to break up a great team like that but Paul was shrewd enough to realise that with his ankle still causing a problem and Gary Neville pushing for a regular place, it was best for him to move elsewhere. I wanted to give him the opportunity to get one last big move and I told him I would not ask for any transfer fee as that may harm his chances of joining the club he wanted.

I know Paul had the chance to join Marseille, at that time the giants of French football, but he ended up going to Derby County, and later Sheffield United and Chelsea. He never really settled anywhere for long after he left United and that is a mark of how much the club meant to him.

Some players can be overawed by the enormity of our club but the challenge of being a Manchester United player brought the best out of Paul. He had the most successful spell of his career here and in my opinion also played the best football of his life in the five trophy-laden years he spent with us.

Old Trafford became his spiritual home and Paul remains a keen supporter to this day. He pops in to my office to see me before games and once joked he speaks to me more now than he did when I was his manager. That is because I class him as a personal friend and he knows I will always be there for him in his time of need. I am somewhat surprised nobody has tapped into his wealth of knowledge in a managerial capacity. I know he has delved into non-league management but for me, he would be an ideal defensive coach at any top Premiership club. Paul is a shrewd observer of the game and could definitely do a sound job for someone.

All in all, I can only say it was a privilege to have worked with Paul and he played a key part in shaping the modern history of the world's greatest club. In fact we are in the process of putting up pictures at the stadium of the best players who have played under me and I have made sure Paul's portrait takes pride of place.

Sir Alex Ferguson
March 2006

Chapter 1

Spot of bother in Italy

ONLY AS our plane taxied slowly towards its terminal resting place from the runway and I looked out at a sea of faces waiting expectantly for our arrival did I realise just what it meant to be part of England's glorious failure to win the World Cup. They were everywhere, fans and well-wishers clinging from every vantage point, waving and bobbing up and down. This was Luton Airport at the end of four and a half momentous weeks in Italy and the roars and shouts greeting us when the plane door finally opened were a colossal shock to those of us in Bobby Robson's Italia 90 squad thinking we would be coming home through a silent, provincial back door.

All this and we had finished fourth, so heaven knows what sort of reception we would have encountered had we actually become the first England side to win the competition since 1966. I struggled down the steps, tired from a long and draining campaign and nursing my double hernia, and it was as much as any of us could do to raise an arm to acknowledge the huge swell of goodwill in front of us. One player said it reminded him of the old film footage of Beatlemania in its heyday and certainly none of us had expected or experienced anything like this.

Once in the airport terminal, and checked through customs, it took us two hours in the team coach to get through the cheering crowds to the sanctuary of our hotel, The Crest, no more than a few hundred yards away. Our driver could not move his vehicle any more than a few yards at a time as fans banged on the sides and screamed for us to wave back. I'm not talking here about children, either, although there were some of those. There were plenty of adults as well, all anxious to make it clear how much they appreciated us, and our efforts on the nation's behalf. Paul Gascoigne played up to it all, donning a giant pair of plastic boobs, sweeping us all along on a tide of Gazzamania, every bit as potent as that experienced by the Beatles.

My bags and those of my team-mates were ripped from my hands by England supporters anxious for souvenirs when at last we were obliged to disembark, find our cars and go home. Being one of the smallest of the squad, I was swamped. People were slapping my back, pulling at my clothes and what little else I was still carrying and it seemed like another couple of hours before I was bundled into my vehicle for the journey back to Wokingham in Berkshire. There was little chance to say goodbye to those among whom I had lived so closely and so intently for the biggest month of my life, it was as much as any of us could do to get away from Luton Airport in one piece. I was shattered by the Italia 90 phenomenon and all I craved was to get home, close my front door and leave the world outside. But there was to be no escape.

As I drove in to our normally quiet little cul-de-sac a street party was already in progress and I was the guest of honour. I had not realised quite how many people lived near me as I stepped out sheepishly among the flags, bunting, balloons and "Welcome home Paul" banners. Gazza would have loved it, but not me. I am retiring by nature and, hard though I tried to join in the fun, I found it all a bit embarrassing. It was as much as I could do to smile my way through the celebrations, sign autographs and appear cheerful.

When at last the final balloon had popped and the party had disbanded, I got inside my house and heaved a sigh so loud it must have been heard in Italy. Only then, as I started to unwind in front of the television, did it dawn on me what we, the England players, had achieved. It's fair to say that it took me a very long time to come down from the 'high' generated by those incredible finals and resume a normal life. For weeks my mind wandered back, again and again, to Sardinia, Cagliari, Turin, Naples and Bologna and I realised just how close I had come to being a World Cup winner. One match stood out above all others. The semi-final against our old rivals, West Germany, will go down as one of the great international matches of all time in terms of the outcome. Even today people talk of the final against West Germany at Wembley in 1966 when a Russian linesman handed England the Jules Rimet Trophy and they talk also of our semi-final in Turin when we were eliminated by the cruellest possible method of penalties after extra time. What a way to settle a semi-final of football's biggest competition. But there is no point in complaining; we all knew the rules.

Our progress to that stage had been far from smooth, struggling to qualify from our group and then needing extra time to beat Belgium and Cameroon. As usual the West Germans had assembled a formidable array of talent and experience but then so had we and, as a relative newcomer to the international side, I had to pinch myself when I stood for the national anthems alongside some of the biggest names ever to grace the game. Here I was on the same pitch as Klinsmann, Voller and Matthaus and as Lineker, Waddle, Gascoigne and Shilton. Paul Parker of Queens Park Rangers did not have quite the same ring about it somehow. My one permanent reminder is a German shirt I swapped at the end of it all with Olaf Thon of Bayern Munich and when I look at it now the memories come racing back. The heat of the night, the passionate crowd, the ecstasy of setting up our equaliser and the agony of penalties.

For the record this was how the two teams lined up. For West Germany there was Bodo Illgner (FC Colgone), Andreas Brehme (Inter Milan), Jurgen Kohler (Bayern), Klaus Augenthaler (Bayern), Thomas Berthold (AS Roma), Guido Buchwald (Stuttgart), Thomas Hassler (Cologne), Lothar Matthaus (Inter Milan), Olaf Thon (Bayern), Rudi Voller (Roma) and Jurgen Klinsmann (Inter Milan). Stefan Reuter of Bayern replaced Hassler and Karl-Heinz Riedle of Werder Bremen took over from Voller as the match progressed. The England side was no less mouth-watering. It was Peter Shilton, Paul Parker, Terry Butcher, Des Walker, Stuart Pearce, David Platt, Mark Wright, Paul Gascoigne, Chris Waddle, Peter Beardsley and Gary Lineker. Trevor Steven took over from Butcher after 72 minutes. Fantastic sides, really, not an apparent weakness and all presided over by two famous coaches. For us there was Bobby Robson, at 57, proven at international level after turning sleepy Ipswich Town into an outstanding club side in the 1970s and 1980s and for the West Germans, the coach was 44-year-old Franz Beckenbauer, on the losing side in 1966 but simply the outstanding midfield player of his generation and venerated the world over. Interestingly also, there was not a player from Arsenal, Chelsea or Manchester United in our team. How times change.

To describe the Germans as efficient sounds like I am poking fun at them, but it's not intended and anyway they had been all the way through the tournament. Having reached the semi-finals, the pressure was off to some extent because there is no disgrace in being beaten in the last four but we were well aware of how the whole of England had been caught up in the frenzy of the World Cup and that in itself created another kind of pressure.

There is no doubt we were apprehensive about them, a glance at the composition of their team justified that, but

I remember the irrepressible Gascoigne breaking the spell. Bobby Robson told him to worry about the world-class Matthaus. "Let him worry about me," said Gazza and that lightened the mood. There is no doubt the Germans were scared of Gazza, and I do mean scared. Gazza was 23 at the time and playing for Tottenham and beginning to look as if he might become one of the greatest players ever produced by England. But he was unreliable, a little volatile and you never knew quite what to expect from him. From the kick off it was clear the Germans had a game plan to wind him up and get him sent off. It was obvious in the way they reacted to his tackles and the way they talked to the referee about him. It worked in the end too, I suppose.

We all remember how Gazza got himself a yellow card as Berthold writhed in mock agony and how Gazza broke down in tears, knowing that the caution would be enough to keep him out of the final. Gazza also had great flair and could find a way through any defence, however efficient, with one piece of individual magic.

The semi-final was an intriguing contest and as it unfurled, I made my first major contribution, picking up the game's first yellow card for a foul after 66 minutes. You could feel the tension, sense the importance of every yard gained in the knowledge that millions around the world were examining every twist and turn as two great footballing nations searched for a priceless advantage. At the heart of it all I could hear Shilton, with the vast knowledge accrued over 124 caps, shouting instructions to his defence and Butcher telling us over the incredible noise generated by a crowd in excess of 62,000 to hold the line, give nothing away.

All went well for an hour and then came an incident for which I shall always be remembered and which will always be debated whenever England and Germany matches are discussed. Was it a Parker own goal? Today, no doubt some "dubious goals panel" would have classed it as such, but I am happy that at the time, it was given to Brehme. Time and again they show the incident on television, Brehme hitting the ball against me at a free kick and it slowly arcing up into the Turin sky and luckily, flukily landing under the bar, leaving Shilton helpless to keep it out.

Let me tell you what really happened. The Germans were given a free kick just outside the area and I was on the right edge of the wall protecting Shilton's goal and at the same time, I thought, giving him plenty of vision. Beardsley was trying to tell me what to do. "Close the ball down," he shouted. I felt that if I had got closer into the wall I would have blocked Shilton's view, so I was caught not quite in the wall and not quite out of it.

Brehme rammed the ball at me and instinctively I turned slightly to protect myself and, I admit in particular, my manly assets. I left a trailing leg, turned my head away and the ball looped off me and over the back-pedalling goalkeeper. One of the most crucial goals in England World Cup history and I was slap, bang in the middle of it.

Television pundit Jimmy Hill gave me a right slagging off for not closing down Brehme, but I took his criticism with a certain amount of contempt because there was a hidden agenda there. I think Hill was still bitter about the way I had left Fulham. It had been in controversial circumstances, as I'll explain later, at a time when he was rescuing the club from a financial crisis and I don't think he had forgiven me. Yes, I should not have turned my back but I defy any man to have charged towards the free kick, his nether regions exposed to a fiercely-struck free kick from a world class player.

I contend, also, that Shilton should have saved it because my partial intervention had taken the pace off the ball, but he was off his line and slow to get back and react. Shilton was an old-school goalkeeper and never shut up, always telling you where your opponent was, even if you knew. In that respect he was precise and articulate and while he was not the best keeper I played with (Schmeichel and Seaman are ahead of him there), his experience was an important part of our defence. As the ball spun downwards, age caught up with Shilton. At 40 years old, the spring in his legs had gone and if he had managed to get off the ground higher than the width of a Rizla paper, he would surely have saved it. No one is decrying what he did for England or for the clubs he represented (125 caps, numerous medals and 1,005 league games) but the general opinion, not just mine, was that he should not have been deceived and beaten in that way. So there we were, an hour gone and one goal down.

I was never noted for my passing even after I had worked so hard to improve it. Get the ball and give it, that was my creed and it served me well. But I did create our equaliser with a pass which Gary Lineker put away with his customary ruthlessness although I am not sure I can claim much credit really if I'm honest. The pass was an ordinary one and Lineker made the best of it, sweeping the ball in with his left foot, but it all helped and I think there was a feeling then that we could now go on and win.

Lineker's goal had come with ten minutes remaining and I suspect we were more ready at that juncture to go the distance than the Germans. People say I was determined to be involved in the England goal to make up for the fact that I had also been involved in the German one, but this was not so. By then I had already been booked for a foul, so one way or another I had certainly made my mark on the match. There was no way we could force a second goal in normal time but going into extra time I felt we were now favourites, because the Germans had been so close to winning through to the final before we had pegged them back, they had to be demoralised.

Over the next 30, strength-sapping minutes I am still convinced we were the better side. But West Germany were full of big names and they proved their worth by showing tremendous resilience. Waddle hit the woodwork and, had that gone in, we would have won, in my view. But that little bit of luck, which had got us through previous rounds, had deserted us and there was an awful inevitability about it being settled on penalties. The final whistle blew and now England's fate rested on what happened over a succession of shots from 12 yards.

As the England players debated in what order we should take our penalties, I took my boots off. There was no way I was going to be involved. My nerves would never have stood such an ordeal and I prayed it would all be settled before I had to put my boots back on and take my turn. I had never taken a spot-kick in my life, not even in training, and the thought of taking one to settle a World Cup semi-final causes me nightmares even now. I reckon it was a toss up between me and Des Walker for the final penalty, neither of us could have been trusted even in an emergency. Shilton was not a great kicker but even he would have been ahead of us in the queue. Luckily, there were better practitioners of the penalty art in our ranks, people like Lineker, Beardsley, Waddle, Pearce and Platt who took them regularly for their clubs and had the bottle to volunteer for such a momentous task in the heat of a battle as intense as this.

Shilton said he felt confident and showed no obvious signs of nerves. His role in the shoot-out was going to be absolutely crucial and, if he was at fault with the German goal, as I insist he was, then this was a great chance to make amends and become a national hero. The drama of this penalty shoot-out began to unfold as I sat and watched.

Lineker put us ahead, Brehme levelled, Beardsley made it 2-1, Matthaus destroyed that advantage, only for Platt to restore it. Suddenly the heat was on the Germans. Karl-Heinz Riedle was next and if he missed this, we would have been in a fantastic position. But he did not, and at 3-3, Stuart Pearce was next in line. We all know what happened next and the sad sequence of events which were to eliminate us. Pearce missed, Thon made it 4-3 to West Germany and then poor old Waddle blazed his effort high on to the terraces. We were out and the German celebrations began.

I will never forget that feeling of devastation, the mind-numbing emptiness that comes with defeat on such a grand scale. We looked at each other, there might have been a tear or two, and there was nothing anyone could have said at that moment which would have raised us. We were out of the World Cup and our dream was over. We had been beaten and there was nothing else to do but accept our fate. The Germans were gracious in victory. I remember Brehme coming over and saying in English how sorry he felt for us but there was nothing for it except to shake their hands and wish them well in the final.

The dressing room was very quiet. What could anyone have said which would have made any difference? There are not many people physically stronger or mentally tougher than Pearce but he was plainly shattered by his failure. I, for one, would never have criticised him because he had to be brave even to take his penalty. Was it pressure? I have never been in that position, so it is hard for me to say, definitely, but someone has to miss eventually and it just happened to be him. Both he and Waddle were normally so reliable and efficient and I hope it did not blight their lives, although I am sure there have been plenty of people down the years who have not been slow to remind them. The coaching staff naturally went to them first to console them as best they could but the only one not apparently overwhelmed was Shilton, our goalkeeper who had got nowhere near any of the four German kicks. Shilton was telling himself and those around him how unlucky he had been because he had guessed the right way every time and had dived accordingly.

But then Pearce broke from his solitary contemplation to shout: "You should have bloody gambled." In my view there was no point in blaming Shilton any more than we should have blamed Pearce or Waddle, but I think we knew what he meant. Shilton had simply followed every kick rather than plunging himself one way or the other when the kick was being taken. Look how Bruce Grobbelaar and Jerzy Dudek won penalty shoot-outs for Liverpool by putting off their opponents, Grobbelaar with his famous rubber legs routine and Dudek by waving his seemingly endless arms. Shilton, in retrospect, should have done something similar but it is easy for me to say that and I am sure he must have thought about it many times since.

Pearce's remark, oddly, broke the silence and there was laughter, much-needed in the circumstances, and we went about the business of cheering up. We had done our best, Robson said how proud he was, and there was nothing else to do but pack up and leave the stadium. Had we lost heavily or put in a poor performance, I am positive we would have been criticised and rightly. But ours was a glorious failure of the kind of which legends are made.

We gave it our best shot and there was no point in dwelling on what might have been. It was after this match that Robson, by now clear in his mind who I was, said of me, I think admiringly: "The little lad jumped like a salmon and tackled like a ferret." Quite a compliment from the man later knighted for his contribution to the game.

I cannot remember feeling any great sense of dejection as we headed back to our hotel. I don't let occasions affect me. My hernia, either side of my groin, was hurting badly and only cortisone injections enabled me to play. I was fortunate to be in the team in the first place and even luckier still to be in by the semi-final, such was the pain. So my overriding emotion, I suppose, was of gratefulness at having played in such a big match. Others may have taken it more personally but if they did, they did not let on.

Despite being out of the tournament, there was one match left for us; the third place play-off against Italy in Bari, for which they were naturally favourites to win and, to be honest, a lot of the heart and purpose had gone out of the tournament for us. It was Shilton's 125th and last England appearance and I, for one, felt Robson should have given a game to his deputy, Chris Woods. Like Schmeichel, Shilton wanted to play in every match, as I suppose we all do when fit, but this was a chance to test Woods, especially as we all knew the World Cup was going to be the end of Shilton's distinguished international contribution. Terry Butcher was not fit enough for a finale to add to his 77 caps, but Woods aside, Robson gave some of our squad members a game and even the disconsolate Neil Webb got 18 minutes at the end.

We lost 2-1 and I am afraid it was me who gave away the penalty winner six minutes from time when I was adjudged, and that is the right word, to have brought down Schillaci. It was not a penalty, as numerous video replays show, but to some extent we were beyond caring and sick of spot-kicks.

Gazza wanted to throw Bobby Robson fully-clothed into the hotel swimming pool later but, typical of him and us, he ripped his toe attempting to do it and was carted off for stitches. Our reward, the same for both sides, was a solid bronze medal. The entire squad got one and it has pride of place among my trophies. Strange to think that in 1966, only the 11 who actually played in the final got a medal. As for the 1990 final, it was hard to watch because I think we knew that if we had played against Argentina we would have beaten them.

The Falklands War had taken place eight years previously and relations between Britain and Argentina were still frosty so there would have been a lot more niggle – and that's saying something when you consider the number of cautions and dismissals and the running battles which littered the final. But the feeling in the England camp was that we would have won. The final, played in Rome on 8th July, was won by the Germans with a goal by Brehme – from the penalty spot.

Broken hearts were soon repaired. Pearce and Waddle got through their mistakes by mental strength and by the firm belief that there was always tomorrow, always another chance to put things right. Both went on to great things at all levels of the game. The spot-kick failures may have hurt them deeply for all we, the rest of the squad, knew but I believe they were redeemed by their professionalism. They had missed penalties before the World Cup semi-final and would do so again. That's what happens when you step up to the plate.

Pearce was a quiet, pleasant man off the pitch, mild-mannered and shy. Waddle was a typical upbeat Geordie and fun to be with. In time they were able to laugh at themselves, taking part in an advert for a pizza which made the most of their lack of penalty success, but they did not hide or look for sympathy. There was not a word of criticism from those of us, like me, not as brave as them and any blame from those at home was based on ignorance or sheer frustration.

Back in Wokingham and in the days before I reported for pre-season training at Queens Park Rangers it was hard to set foot outside my house without someone wanting to talk through that semi-final, that shoot-out. They still do, but now I can look at it all dispassionately and with the wonderful benefit of hindsight. It was a fabulous competition to be part of and I can say, without a doubt, that it made my career.

I was now an established international, an established First Division footballer with a good salary and a way of life beyond my wildest dreams a few short years previously. Aged 26 I was approaching my best years and in quiet moments to myself after our return to England I was able to look back on how it had all started.

Chapter 2

Fulham's East-Ender

BY RIGHTS I should have been a West Ham man, my blood running with claret and blue. I was born within spitting distance of Upton Park at Forest Gate, and West Ham were the dominant team of that part of East London. But for me they meant nothing because, as the son of Jamaican parents, their attitude to black players during the time I was growing up in the 1960s and 1970s was little short of hostile.

I remember making a rare visit to Upton Park to watch the Hammers against, ironically, Manchester United and it was an experience I will never be able to forget. I stood with my pals on the closely packed terraces and, bearing in mind I was about 13 or 14 at the time and barely five feet tall, I was kicked and pushed by West Ham fans and told to get out the way. There was incessant chanting aimed at the few black players then on the pitch, bananas were thrown and it was a frightening and unnerving experience.

A few years later, when I was 16 and still not much bigger than five feet, I was at right-back in Fulham's youth team and we played West Ham in the South East Counties League at Chadwell Heath. My direct opponent was Bobby Barnes, a black lad who had a few games in their first team later. Standing on the touchline was Eddie Baily, in charge of the West Ham side and eminent within football as former number two at Tottenham to Double-winner Bill Nicholson. Baily gave Barnes a non-stop barrage of abuse, shouting "you can get past that coon", and other even less flattering references to mine and Barnes' blackness. Every time I saw Baily after that I cringed. How George Parris and other blacks coming through the West Ham youth system tolerated that atmosphere I don't know. Clyde Best deserved his medal.

Yet, for the first few years of my life, this was home, an area of London full of immigrants like my parents, Louis and Myra. Dad came from the St Catherine district of Jamaica in 1959 and mum came from St James parish two years later, typical of the huge numbers of West Indians who came to Britain at that time, encouraged by the prospect of a better life and the promise of plenty of work. Dad worked in a foundry and mum was a nurse but for 12 years she was a traffic warden around Chancery Lane in Central London. Three times irate motorists ended up in court because they tried to run her over.

Life was not easy for Caribbean immigrants. They came over by the boat-load from the sunshine of the West Indies to Britain's grey streets to work on the railways and to be nurses. I understand that from other islands, the British government paid the fares of the newcomers and these were paid back out of their wage packets once they had settled and found jobs. But, for some reason, this was not the case with Jamaicans, as my mum found out the hard way.

She was working at a Lyons corner shop in Whitechapel, her first job in England, when she spilled a customer's tea by accident. The angry customer called her a black so-and-so and in her fury, mum ripped off her pinny, buttons popping, and resigned on the spot. But another waitress said to her "you can't give up, you have to pay back your ticket". When mum said she had no fare to pay back, she discovered how men and women from elsewhere in the Caribbean had the burden of paying for the privilege of coming to England week by week until the government had been reimbursed.

Now I would be eligible to play for Jamaica, but there were no such thoughts as I grew up and I only ever wanted to play for England. The nearest I have ever been to Jamaica was a holiday in St Lucia in 1996 and, like the children of most post-war immigrants, I have no real empathy with my parents' background. It must have been tough for my mum and dad bringing up a family of four in such circumstances, knowing that many of the whites among whom they lived were intrinsically against them.

Mum remembers how the National Front tried to sell her one of their magazines outside Upton Park. Rising to her full height of 4ft 11ins, she told them where to put it. I like to think relations in that part of London and elsewhere have improved but at that time, there was an undercurrent of racism which made life difficult for the newcomers and their children.

It was always difficult at school where I was one of the few black children and just as difficult socially. When I was 17 or 18 I recall going to a pub in Dagenham, deep in West Ham and National Front territory, and black taxi drivers coming in to call for fares were routinely abused. One bloke leant across and said to me, reassuringly: "Don't worry, son, you're one of us."

We moved a little further out of the East End to Romford, not a million miles away, and then to Rainham in Essex. Doreen is the oldest of us four children and the only girl. Doreen was athletic and quick and excelled at hurdles and sprinting and of my two younger brothers, Denis might have made a living out of sport had he possessed the drive and determination to match his talent. I think it is fair to say Denis did not push himself when he was briefly at Southend but he later played with some distinction for Dagenham and Rainham. Denis was a taller version of me to some extent and because we look similar was even known to sign autographs on my behalf when I was at Fulham. He now delivers water bottles.

If only I had had Colin's physique. Colin was a builder and is now a doorman. When it came to dishing out the family height and weight I missed out because Colin got it all. But he was not interested in sport while the limit of dad's involvement in games was to take a few cans of his native island's home brew, Red Stripe, and bang them together supportively while watching the West Indies on television playing cricket. Like my mum, he was extremely proud of me playing football for England and slightly bemused that I went so far in the game because there was no history of sporting prowess in the family back in Jamaica. Dad loved his cricket, as they all did, but that was about it.

The less said about my school career, the better. Until I was 16 I attended, if that's the right word, Saunders Drapers Comprehensive in Hornchurch but not with any enthusiasm. I did not enjoy school. In fact I hated it. My concentration was poor and I lived only for football or for PE lessons. Basketball and gymnastics were my main interests and it more than made up for the tedium of the more formal subjects. Just before I left aged 16 I sat three CSE subjects: English, maths and geography. To this day I have no idea if I passed. I feared the worst. I always say I took English to read road signs, maths to find out how far I had to go and geography so that I knew where I was. There was some interest in metalwork but then again, I have found over the years how useless I am at DIY.

Cross-country took place on cold Saturday mornings and while I was a capable distance runner I had no great interest in it. I used to implore my mum to write me sick notes and when she quite rightly refused on principle I would get my sister to do it instead. My favourite distance was 800 metres because I had a strong finish and I was good enough to represent Essex. I also represented Essex at basketball but not, strangely, at football. I say strangely but even as a teenager I was barely five feet tall and all skin and bone.

Representative football teams were full of big lads, some of them already built like adults, and little guys like me were not considered. Even though there was a perfectly reasonable school 600 yards from our home and my sister went to it, I was sent nearly three miles away to that Hornchurch comprehensive where I found I was one of the few blacks. On pretty much the first day, a white kid grabbed me and showed me on his lapel one of those Robertson jam golliwogs and shoved it in my face with the menacing words: "See that, that's what happened to the last black here."

Some teachers attempted to understand and help, others did not. I remember Mr Cole, the careers' officer, pouring scorn on me when I told him I wanted to be a footballer. "You have got a one in a thousand chance," he told me when I was about 14. "Even then it is not guaranteed." Mr Murray was different. Hard but fair, he encouraged me and Colin when he arrived at the school in my third year and made me feel that perhaps, against the odds, I might yet become a footballer.

Hornchurch was then predominantly white but my path at school was all the smoother for my athletic prowess. Being sporty, life was easier. Football was my passion and it was all I ever wanted to do in life, be a professional player, and in fairness no one ever tried to tell me it would not happen. From the age of eight I was a striker but it became apparent that if I was to progress in the game it would have to be as a defender. At all levels I preferred the game in front of me. But for whom I was going to play was another matter. Mum used to do her shopping at Tesco in West Ham. While she did so, dad went to the pub to play dominoes and the best part of it was that once mum had finished shopping she took us for a burger, chips and Knickerbocker Glory; all this in the shadow of Upton Park. But West Ham were not interested in me and I was not interested in them.

Tottenham were the team for me at that time. Being born in April 1964 I had missed the Double-winners of course but they were still a formidable outfit and my particular idol was the Irish goalkeeper Pat Jennings. I am not sure, even now, why it was that I held Jennings in such high esteem but there was a presence about him I liked. I used to get to White Hart Lane early and stand on 'The Shelf' to get a vantage point to see him, Steve Perryman, Martin Chivers, Joe Kinnear and Peter Taylor. I have never met Jennings but even recently I stood in awe like some star-struck teenager when I spotted him at Belfast Airport. I didn't have the nerve to introduce myself.

I also watched non-league sides Dagenham and Enfield among big, intense crowds. When the sides met in derby matches there were invariably arrests and it was as dramatic, in its way, as any local rivalry. My favourites were Peter Burton, a Billericay teacher who played for Dagenham, and Dennis Moore, a top-class centre-half. I'm sure they could have played in the Football League, they certainly had the ability, but in those days there was not the financial incentive to give up a good job and enter the precarious world of the professional game.

I was a tiny 11-year-old when my own possibilities of becoming a professional became something more realistic than a childish fantasy. I played for a team called Pegasus in Hornchurch before I was taken to Romford Juniors by Johnny Martin, the club's coach and father of Steve, one of my present-day best friends (I'm godfather to his eldest daughter). Romford Juniors had a reputation for being the best team in the area for children of my age and we regularly attracted scouts from professional clubs to our games on Sundays. Steve Tapp, who later had a couple of games for Fulham, was a contemporary while I used to play against the striker Dean Coney when he turned out for Barking and Dagenham.

Fulham were particularly active in our area though they were by no means a big club and were based on the other side of London. The place should have been crawling with scouts from West Ham, Tottenham, Arsenal, Leyton Orient even, but Johnny was a Fulham scout and pushed a few of us in their direction. I'm glad he did. The Cottagers, as they were known, had a scout by the name of Dennis Taylor who spotted my potential while Del Quigley was also involved when I signed affiliated forms in 1976, a mere 11 years old and with stars in my eyes.

So organised were Fulham that they even had a training school in Dagenham and although I could walk the one and a half miles there, I claimed expenses for my bus fare. I look back on that little ruse as my first football pay packet. Fulham took us East End boys to Craven Cottage and to the club's training ground at Roehampton where we played a few matches and got a taste of what we all hoped would be the life to come. It was a day out on the train, if nothing else, but I liked the feel of Fulham and came to regard them as my club, cementing the relationship further in 1978 when I became an associate schoolboy.

Forget the school bit of that last word. There was only one thing I wanted to be and school had nothing to do with it. I may only have been 14 but if I could have left school there and then I would have done. I was a right-back by now and opponents still looked terrifyingly huge to me but my determination to succeed as a footballer was as strong as it had ever been. What I lacked in height I made up for in pace, tackling ability and tenacity.

It was the 1979/80 season and I understand I made my South East Counties League debut against a Norwich side containing the six-feet-plus John Fashanu, although I have to say I don't remember it. Fashanu would have been a foot taller than me and there were similar discrepancies when we played other sides. Terry Mancini, the former Republic of Ireland defender but very much a Cockney, was the youth team coach and I know he had reservations not about my ability but about my size. It was a physical league and many of the boys were 18 and looked like grown-ups to a minute 15-year-old still, reluctantly, at school. Terry was very direct and said what he felt and soon made me aware that I was attempting to enter a serious business.

Millwall were the team to beat in this league and there I came across Kevin O'Callaghan, Dean Horrix, Andy Massey, Paul Roberts, Keith Stevens and Alan McLeary. All of them went on to have significant careers and it was a chastening experience facing them in the same youth team. I came off blacker than I was already.

Mancini's concern about my size was shared by Bobby Campbell, the club manager. Bobby was a loud Liverpudlian and I know he was not always popular because he could be aggressive and abrasive but I liked him and he liked me. Perhaps it was because I was cute, barely five feet tall, but he always made a point of saying hello and goodbye and making me, the humblest of associate schoolboys, feel welcome. He even threw out Les Strong, the stalwart left-back, from one first-team meeting so that I could sit in on it.

But such was their worry about me growing that I was sent to the Westminster Hospital on the Embankment for tests on my bones. I had inherited my mother's stature and I knew I would never be tall unless I shot up in my late teens. Fulham wanted to know exactly how tall I could expect to be at maturity. Campbell was as relieved as me and my parents when I was told by specialists that I could expect to grow to a more acceptable maximum of 5ft 8ins although I only ever got as far as 5ft 7ins. They said that boys often did not stop growing until they were 21, leaving me five or six years to develop. Had the news been less encouraging I might well have been informed, as so many had been in the past: "Sorry son, you are not going to be big enough."

In January 1980, school and I parted company and in May of that year, the suitably reassured Fulham offered me an apprenticeship which I gratefully accepted. It was the same month that the first team were relegated to the Third

Division but I never had any doubts that I had made the right decision. Fulham's investment in youth was about to pay off. Coney, Jeff Hopkins, Dale Tempest, Cliff Carr, John Marshall and Peter Scott all signed the same forms at the same time and all went on to become key players for the club in the 1980s.

My first season on the staff, 1980/81, was one of turmoil after Campbell's transfer wheeling and dealing, while making a healthy profit, had done nothing for the stability of the squad and cost him his job in October 1980. In his place came Malcolm Macdonald, a former England international, a legend on Tyneside, but finished as a player at 29 because of knee injuries at a time when he should have been at his peak. Macdonald was a man in a hurry, still I think coming to terms with his premature retirement.

"You are looking after my boots," was his first demand of me. They were Adidas with long studs and when you get an order like that from the manager you obey. Macdonald was a strong guy physically and mentally, he knew what he wanted and he could be ruthless. Supermac was also an awesome trainer, approaching each five-a-side match with the same fierce commitment he had shown in his playing prime. None of us wanted to be in his team because we were scared of the way he barked instructions. His frustration and anger were evident as he screamed "give me the ball" and, believe me, we did.

Les Strong called him Sammy after Sammy Chung, the former Wolves manager who had a Chinese background. Macdonald's high cheekbones did give him a Chinese quality.

Macdonald was born near Fulham's ground and was converted from right-back to centre forward by Bobby Robson and he was a fearsome striker in his day, worshipped at Newcastle and respected and feared by opponents the length of England. At Newcastle they still revere him in the same way they revere Jackie Milburn and Alan Shearer.

After his million-pound move to Arsenal, he became one of the great swashbuckling centre forwards of his day, fast, determined and brave. Not a tall man by any means, Macdonald had bandy legs and great power. In 14 internationals in four years from 1972, Supermac scored six goals, five of them in one match. Only injuries stopped him playing more. Those injuries were still evident after his retirement because at the end of every training session which he approached with the same commitment as an international, his knees swelled like balloons.

I believe he could have been just as big a manager as he was a player. On a shoestring he began to transform Fulham, getting us out of the Third Division and nearly into the first before an indiscretion led to an unjust sacking. Had he stayed, who knows what he might have gone on to achieve.

Macdonald was married with five daughters but a spot of marital infidelity with a woman at a hotel proved to be his undoing. Today it would not have provoked much reaction. It would have been seen as a private, domestic problem but our chairman Ernie Clay was a family man and did not like his club being associated with such outrage and that was the end of Supermac at Craven Cottage. Malcolm was different. He liked a brandy and he liked the short, stumpy cigars, Rios as they are known. There were always boxes of them on the back window ledge of his Citroen Safari.

I shall always be thankful to Malcolm because it was he who gave me my league debut after only nine reserve team matches in the penultimate Third Division game of the season at home to Reading. Coney had already played in the first team and Hopkins was to follow soon afterwards as evidence of the new Fulham emerging under Macdonald.

My starting chance came on 25th April 1981. I was just 17 and a crowd, if that is the right word, of 4,601 saw us lose 2-1. I must by then have been all of 5ft 1in and as Reading lined up, Kerry Dixon at centre forward and Lawrie Sanchez left midfield, I thought I was in the land of the giants. My direct opponent was the experienced Mike Kearney and while he never said anything, he must have been rolling about laughing when he saw me up against him. I remember shaking with nerves beforehand and it must have transmitted itself on the pitch but there were no obvious blunders and I was away. For the record, the Fulham side was Jim Stannard, me, Les Strong, John Beck, Geoff Banton, Gary Peters, Gordon Davies, Brian Greenaway, Coney, Sean O'Driscoll (sub Ron Goodlass) and Ray Lewington.

Much as Macdonald was a good influence, the man behind my gradual development was undoubtedly Ray Harford. I believe he was the real reason for Fulham's recovery. Barry Simmonds and Tony Banfield had been and gone as youth coaches and it was Macdonald who brought him in from Colchester to oversee this group of young lads who were coming through the ranks together.

Ray was my mentor as was, in her way, Maureen his wife. Ray liked me as a player and person and there was mutual respect but he was always straight with me and always told the truth, however unpalatable it might have been. At that time, with my debut behind me, I imagine I thought I had already made the grade. Unlike Jeff Hopkins, who always gave 100 per cent in training and in matches and could be relied upon, the same could not be said for me. Ray called me an enigma which, for about a week, I thought was another way of calling me a nigger before I was told what it meant. Ray was as blunt as he could be when he said Macdonald could not trust me because my attitude was wrong.

Even in Campbell's day, I was a poor, poor trainer. I hated the stop-start aspect of preparing set pieces and I found it almost impossible to absorb any information. Mike Kelly, Campbell's assistant, once gave me a terrible rollicking. We were training at Roehampton. He was a goalkeeper by trade and we were supposed to be working on keeping possession with the keeper throwing the ball out to the nearest defender to build moves from the back. Nothing went right. Every time the ball was thrown to me by him it bounced on a, I have to say, uneven surface over my foot or under it. The harder I tried the worse it got and the more irate Kelly became. Kelly slaughtered me like a sergeant-major with raw recruits on a drill ground and with very good reason.

I was just not concentrating and that was always my problem. I only ever wanted to be playing in a game, five a-side or whatever. Kelly later became England goalkeeping coach in the 1990 World Cup when, of course, I was playing and we laughed about those awful days when I could do no right. I never expected him to be England's keeper coach and I am equally sure he never thought I would play for England.

If Campbell was Mr Nice Guy with me, Kelly in those far off days at Fulham, was Mr Nasty. If Mike Kelly took a training session, I was genuinely frightened. Luckily, I took the hint and set about improving. It was all about fighters, said Ray Harford, and the non-league game was full of people with plenty of ability but had the wrong mentality. I was determined not to be one of them.

Ray went on to manage Blackburn and Wimbledon, when they were in the top flight, and as Kenny Dalglish's number two I know he deserves a share of the credit for helping Blackburn win the championship. His public persona did not match that known to his friends. Many people thought him dull and dour but that was far from true. He could be very funny, compassionate and kind and I spoke to him regularly long after I moved to Queens Park Rangers. His early death was a big blow to me and those of us who knew the real Ray Harford.

At around this time I met my first wife, Wendy. She was Jeff Hopkins' sister's best friend and we met at a party for Peter Nott, a Fulham contemporary who sadly did not reach the first team. Wendy and I went out together for five years before marrying in 1987. We divorced in 1995 but our daughter, Georgie, is close to me and was 18 in April 2006. But until I was 19 I was living at home and getting the benefit of mum's cooking and, while I was given no special diet to follow by the Westminster Hospital specialists, I was growing taller slowly but discernibly.

The next landmark for any young aspiring footballer is to be offered your first professional contract. This I got when I was 18 in 1982 but it was by no means guaranteed. Looking back, I was a little lucky because Macdonald did not think he could rely on me and felt I was over-dependent on my natural ability and my pace. I knew some negative things were being said about me but he left it to Harford to lay it on the line. Harford told me I needed to ally my talent to a desire and purpose which he felt had been lacking. For a start I could begin to take training a lot more seriously. It's true that all I was interested in was playing a game, I was bored to tears by set play practice and I was without any focus or concentration. I realise now that my first pro contract could well have been my last and it is Harford who got me through it and took me on to a different level. In retrospect I owe him a lot.

In 1981/82, I played in five more league matches, two of them in the starting line-up, but in many respects I was still a youth and at that level I was gaining a reputation for something other than laziness. How humble Fulham got invited, I don't know, but we took part in a youth tournament in Lloret de Mar in which the cream of Feyenoord, Real Madrid and Barcelona also played. We drew with Barcelona and lost narrowly to Real Madrid in the final. My trip abroad ended on a sour personal note. My straw donkey, the obligatory souvenir in those days, broke on the airport luggage conveyor belt. Macdonald acknowledged my development in his programme notes: "Paul Parker has a tremendous future in football because he is not only an effective destroyer in defence but he is also a very creative player."

I have to say I am not sure I deserved the "creative" part at that stage of my career. I was obviously winning over Macdonald and, if I was, Harford's message was the inspiration. I must also have impressed others outside the club because, out of the blue, Harford informed me one day that I had been chosen to play for England Youth. I played against Scotland from the start and was substitute in two other matches. My first taste was as a substitute against Sweden and the team that day was Andy Gosney (Portsmouth), Frank Yallop (Ipswich), Ian Templeton (Ipswich), Paul Elliott (Charlton), Stewart Robson (Arsenal), Kevin Gage (Wimbledon), Martin Singleton (Coventry), Ray Walker (Aston Villa), Danny Wallace (Southampton), Geoff Dey (Sheffield United) and Mark Schiavi (West Ham). Used subs were me, Gary Childs of West Bromwich and Jimmy Gilligan of Watford. John Pearson of Sheffield Wednesday and Mark Walters (Aston Villa) were in the side on my full debut. It says something about the high casualty rate among even the best of youth players that so few went on to make a mark on the game.

John Cartwright was the manager and the Uruguayan Danny Bergera was his coach. But of all those players I was the only one to go on and play regularly for England at senior level. Wallace and Walters became one-cap wonders and several went on to have solid, lower-division careers but at the time Robson stood out and Elliott was a big strong centre-half who won everything in the air. How sad that injury blighted their careers because at youth level they were outstanding. As for Geoff Dey, I cannot, for the life of me, recall him.

For my own part, I had a feeling it did nothing to make me think any less of myself, especially as I was the only Third Division player. I began to think I was something a bit special and Macdonald went on record to say I was the best defensive brain at Fulham. Macdonald likened me to Billy Bremner, which was some accolade, although I could not see the similarity and I preferred it when Bobby Robson compared me with Nobby Stiles. I mean no disrespect to either man, far from it.

When I was an apprentice at Fulham, Ian Snodin was a mate of mine and playing for Doncaster where Bremner was manager. I went to stay with Ian at a time when Doncaster were called in for pre-season training a week before I was due to start at Fulham. I thought it would be a good opportunity to get a few days under my belt before reporting to Fulham. Billy made us run up hills and South Yorkshire slag heaps to get us fit. I was violently sick at the top of one such slag heap. We did not see those in Roehampton.

When it came to piggy-in-the-middle, as we call it, the game aimed at retaining possession, Bremner was fantastic. His one and two touches were still incredible and way above those of us around him. As for Nobby, hero of the 1966 World Cup win, he was something of a role model. Nobby was a ball-winner, scared of no one bigger than himself and a great destroyer. I saw myself as being similar and I was an inch taller.

My immediate goal was to get a regular spot in the Fulham defence at right-back, central defender or sweeper. Jeff Hopkins was at right-back, Roger Brown and Tony Gale were the central defence and the durable Strong was at left-back. My mate Jeff was in my way but I can understand with retrospect why he was preferred. You always knew what you were going to get from Jeff, who went on to play for Wales and is now coaching in Australia. Jeff was aggressive, sometimes too aggressive but he was tall, lean and could lump it down the pitch when required. Harford told me not to lose heart, that Jeff's attitude was better and that he was in the team for a reason.

Not that I played much part, it was a good season for the club. We were promoted in third place behind Carlisle and

Burnley and, to Supermac's great delight, beat Newcastle in the League Cup. Roger Brown got us up when he scored against Lincoln at the end of the season to get us the point we needed. Big Roger was a character. A late entrant to the game, blond Roger came to us from Bournemouth for £50,000 and was a formidable defensive barrier. He was signed on a Friday, the day before we were due to play Chelsea.

My first sight of him was on the day he signed at Roehampton, drinking brandy with Macdonald and sharing a packet of his cigars. Can you imagine that happening today? But he gave good value and was never scared to get hurt. One clash with the equally intimidating Tony Cunningham of Lincoln ended with both cutting their eyes in a fierce encounter but Roger relished that sort of challenge and I was always glad he was on my side.

So there I was, an England Youth international, newly professional and now a part of a club promoted to the Second Division thanks to the efforts of others. I don't remember plotting my career, as such, but I think I was aware that I could make a decent living out of football. My school days were long behind me and all I needed was a chance to hold down a place in the Fulham side. That was my immediate ambition but I was made to wait for my opportunity. Manchester United and World Cups looked a long way off in 1982.

Chapter 3

Rites of passage

MATCHES AGAINST Liverpool were always intense, often bitter affairs when I was at Manchester United but two against Liverpool when I was at Fulham provided important landmarks in my career. The first alerted the outside world to my potential, the second told me it was time to move on.

It was in the 1983/84 season and I was holding down a regular place and playing with the confidence of someone who knew they had served their apprenticeship and learned their lessons. I played in most of the matches and although we failed to mount a promotion challenge, finishing 11th, the highlight was a series of three against Bob Paisley's all-conquering side in the League Cup. In those days there were no sudden death penalties and we carried on replaying until such time as someone won outright.

Malcolm Macdonald took the bold decision to drop our club captain, Roger Brown, and play me in the centre of defence for my greater mobility alongside the developing Tony Gale. Kevin Lock's penalty earned us a replay at Craven Cottage and then Lock scored another spot-kick at Anfield to bring them back for a second replay. Unfortunately I damaged knee ligaments in the first replay after colliding with Craig Johnston and was unable to play in the second but I served notice in the previous two matches of my ability on a national scale. I recall Steve Stammers, then of the *Daily Star*, gave me rave reviews so, looking back, I think this was my first big break. I had gained a profile.

Liverpool had a wonderful side in those days with people like Grobbelaar, Kennedy, Neal, Lawrenson, Hansen, Dalglish, Rush and Souness so to play well against them, as I did, got a few people sitting up having been alerted to my potential. Dalglish was my direct opponent and I kept him quiet just by marking him tightly, not letting him turn and I think he might have been surprised by my doggedness. But the Fulham team was strong in those days and we all did our jobs.

Liverpool won the second replay in extra time and I could only watch from the stands but it was just the exposure I needed. Paisley did not miss many tricks and I found out subsequently that he had bid £200,000 for me. Not having an agent, as even the humblest of players do now, there was nothing I could do about it. In fact I only found out about it through reading the papers and it never crossed my mind to pursue the matter. Ernie Clay, our chairman, loved Fulham and wanted us to be strong, strong enough to get promoted and face Liverpool on a regular basis. So he rejected it.

While I was proud to be associated with a club as massive as Liverpool, I remember feeling a little annoyed that I had not been consulted, though not annoyed enough to go marching into the chairman's office and slap a newspaper down on his desk. Who knows what would have happened had Mr Clay accepted. It got me wondering about the future, though, because where Liverpool had failed others might one day succeed. I was also a little apprehensive because the prospect of leaving my home area did not greatly appeal.

By now, thanks to the coaching I was receiving and partly because I was maturing as a player and as a person, I was beginning to evolve and develop a technique and I was not slow to take advantage of the fact that I was often much smaller than my opponents when I played in the centre of defence. I discovered that naturally I had a good spring in my feet which meant that I could compete in the air with players much taller than myself.

The secret was in the timing but also in knowing how to block off the man I was marking by positioning and stopping them using their advantage to get clean headers. I was using my brain and my cunning and I was not slow to squeeze sympathy from referees who tended to favour me if ever there was a clash because I was so small for a central defender. They looked on me leniently and saw the bigger men as bullies and I have to say I won a lot of free kicks that way, many more than I should have done. Anyway, the bigger or better known my opponent the more determined I was to get the better of them.

Another abiding memory of those matches against Liverpool is how nervous I was before the games. I suppose I was bound to be affected, considering my age, and I came to realise later how important it was to be a little nervous to give you an edge. Every player is affected, or at least they should be, but some cope better than others and everyone has a different way of dealing with those butterflies fluttering around in the stomach. For instance, Terry Butcher was rowdy and loud, shouting in the dressing room to psyche himself up, Paul Ince used to kick a ball against a wall incessantly, Eric Cantona used to disappear into a world of his own, talking to no one and Alan McDonald, a great centre-half at Queens Park Rangers, broke all today's accepted rules by disappearing into a toilet for a quick cigarette.

We all had our ways of dealing with the build-up of pressure. Mine was to stay quiet but I only wish I had been like Mark Hughes who always appeared to have nerves of steel; nothing seemed to bother him and he was so relaxed any outsider would have thought he was not due to play. Most players will tell you that once on the pitch nerves tend to disappear but I came across some who took their hesitancy on to the pitch and that can be fatal.

I showed nerves of a different kind at Derby where I was rammed, literally, at the end of one vital match for both sides. It was in the 1982/83 season when I was still an occasional member of the side with 22 appearances in all, and the team under Macdonald's flamboyant leadership were at one stage third in the table in a promotion place ten points clear of the club in fourth place. It began to look as if Supermac was about to take us to our second promotion but we hit a bad patch (nerves again) and it all went down to the final match of the season at Derby in front of a passionate Baseball Ground crowd.

Derby needed to win to stay up and we needed to win to get promoted so it was hardly surprising the stadium was like a cauldron. We lost by a single goal, thereby allowing Leicester to sneak the final promotion spot by a point. I was substitute and a little glad not to be on the pitch as the crowd began to encroach in anticipation of the final whistle. Robert Wilson, a Fulham team-mate, was punched and kicked attempting to take a throw and I think the referee panicked by calling a halt some 78 seconds early. As players from both sides rushed for the tunnel, it became apparent that the referee was not alone in panicking.

Derby are not known as the Rams for nothing and in those days paraded a ram around the pitch as their mascot. The poor creature obviously became frightened in the mayhem as fans poured forward hysterically and everyone on the team benches fled for their safety. I was among those trying to get to the sanctuary of the dressing room when the ram did what all rams do in moments of crisis and charged head first at the nearest object. In this case, it was me. He butted my legs and gave me a nasty graze or two. Jeff Hopkins got to the dressing room later covered in cuts and bruises and with his shirt all but ripped off only to find it was me, an unused sub, who was getting treatment for being savaged by a sheep. Not an injury easily explained in footballing terms.

Malcolm Macdonald had by now begun to build a reputation as a manager every bit as formidable as that he had achieved as a player. He was one point away from getting us into the First Division and had he done so, who knows what might have happened to him. But then came his sacking on the threshold of a possible big career in management and Fulham were never the same again all the while I was at Craven Cottage.

None of the players thought he should have been fired but the chairman did what he felt was right and as a club we went backwards fast. His departure took away so much from the club because he had an aura about him which inspired loyalty and a determination to succeed on his behalf. The whole atmosphere changed immediately and we went on a sort of rollercoaster ride, good one day, bad the next. Without him, I think the whole club lost its way and the momentum he had built up over one promotion and one near miss evaporated almost overnight.

His next move was not in management elsewhere, as it should have been, but to run a pub in Worthing and to all intents and purposes he was lost to the game, to the great regret of those who had played for him. On a personal level, he had shown enough faith in me to give me my debut and to get me training like a proper professional. Without him and the perseverance of one or two others, I suppose I might also have been lost to football at this level.

While I was by now a better trainer, I can't honestly say I ever enjoyed the daily ritual of getting fit, even at Manchester United or with England. Pre-season was a nightmare and I used to have sleepless nights thinking about it the week before we were due to report at the height of summer. Only in the last few days would I attempt to go on a run or two to get some condition back into the legs and I never repeated my Doncaster experience.

Some players really gave training everything. I never in my life met anyone who trained as hard as Gavin Peacock at Queens Park Rangers. His commitment was incredible. Mark Dennis gained a reputation as a hard man but he had this great willingness to win even if he took it too far sometimes and was no less forthright in training sessions. Gary Stevens, the former Everton full-back, was top-class in his preparations and I understand among present players Gary Neville takes his fierce pride of performance on to the training ground. I did what I had to, but there were others who did not train with any great gusto at all.

Mark Hughes was by no means the best trainer and when it came to selecting teams for five-a-side matches he was always the last pick. This might come as a surprise to those who remember him as a terrific player, a strong man and ferocious competitor but when it came to kick-arounds, he was a liability, always trying dainty flicks and not taking it as seriously as he should have done. I wonder if he allows such antics now that he is a manager. Brian McClair was the same. We laughed at them at the time but we always knew that once we were on the pitch and involved in a match, they would give everything all of the time and were 100 per cent professional. But then again, if I were to be judged on my training performances no one would have chosen me.

The best coach in terms of training I ever came across in 20 years was Brian Kidd. This again might surprise a few people but that is what I thought of him. Brian kept things simple and basic in the knowledge that if you were a Manchester United player, you were there on merit. It was assumed you were a top-class player. Brian liked short, sharp sessions, always different and stimulating, and there was never any time to relax, get cold or let your mind get lazy. We moved swiftly from one discipline to another when he took training and even I actually looked forward to his sessions. I felt he took coaching on to a different level because he respected and believed in us as Manchester United players and expected in return a level of performance above the ordinary.

In the lower divisions, as I found at Fulham and Queens Park Rangers, the players were self-evidently not as good. There was therefore a much greater emphasis on endurance, physical strength and organisation. We were taught how to defend at corners and free kicks and taught how to attack at set pieces, where to stand, when to run and what to do. Outside the Premiership this is very important. At Manchester United, while not ignoring such aspects as set pieces, it was assumed by Kidd and other coaches that we had by definition the ability to improvise and use our skill and wits. That was why Manchester United had bought us.

Ray Harford became Fulham manager in May 1984 and much as it grieves me to say it, the club's decline accelerated with his appointment. Not because we did not like him or because he was in any way bad at his job. Far from it, we did like him and he was a good coach. The problem was that we all liked him and did not respect him in the same way as a manager. When a manager is fired or goes, players always want his number two to be promoted. Better the devil you know, I suppose, but it does not always make for progress.

Looking back, we let him down. We became too comfortable, bordering on the complacent and we did not respect him in quite the way we should have done. A good manager cannot be liked by all the players. Only 11 can start and in Ray's case I think we might have taken him for granted. He never had the same hold of us as Macdonald, who was a little feared, and our individual and team performances were at best patchy.

Our inconsistency was exemplified in one extraordinary match at Portsmouth on New Year's Day 1985. In a howling gale sweeping across the pitch I was not alone in defending like a novice in the first half in the teeth of the wind and when the whistle blew for the break we were lucky to be only 4-0 down. I hid behind a pillar in the Fratton Park dressing room at half-time to avoid the rollicking I should have received from Harford. But in the second half with the wind behind us we clawed it back to 4-4 thanks to a late penalty from Kevin Lock and if the game had gone on five minutes longer I have no doubt we would have won. Portsmouth fans were furious, the players shell-shocked and we celebrated like we had achieved a momentous victory.

Years later, playing for United, I was on the receiving end of a similar comeback. We were three up against Liverpool only for Neil Ruddock to head in a cross to earn them a draw. It was not a nice feeling.

By the time of the Portsmouth match I was an England Under-21 international having made my debut against Finland not far up the road from Portsmouth at the Dell, home of Southampton on 16th October 1984. The match was significant also as the scene of my first goal. I had not even scored a league goal then. Chris Waddle scored the first in front of 6,325 people and I got the second, a right-footed shot from 20 yards. It was one of the best seen at Southampton until a certain Matt Le Tissier came along. At least, that is what I tell myself. The team that night was David Seaman (Birmingham), Barry Venison (Sunderland), me, Paul Elliott (Luton), Ian Cranson (Ipswich), Gary Shelton (Sheffield Wednesday), Stewart Robson (Arsenal), Trevor Steven (Everton), Paul Rideout (Aston Villa), Waddle and Danny Wallace, the local boy. Tony Cottee replaced Wallace and Alan Dickens of West Ham came on for Shelton. Only about half a dozen of those went on to play for England and only three of us were black.

I felt slightly inferior, not because I was one of the few blacks, but because I was one of the few players from outside the First Division. In my other five appearances for the Under-21s that season, there was only me, Seaman and later Bobby Mimms and Ian Snodin who came from lower division clubs and we tended to stick together as a sort of clique. My other appearances were against Turkey, Israel, Republic of Ireland, Romania and Finland again and I was playing at right-back while for Fulham I was a central defender.

I did not mind where I played in defence. I was a defender by nature, attacking never appealed to me and although I think I could perhaps have contemplated playing in midfield for Fulham and Queens Park Rangers, I could not have done for United. I was not sure enough of my skill and I liked the game to be played in front of me.

Gradually the Fulham team built by Malcolm Macdonald was dismantled around me. Roger Brown (Norwich) and Tony Gale (West Ham), outstanding central defenders, were sold and Ray Houghton (Oxford), Robert Wilson (Huddersfield), Sean O'Driscoll (Bournemouth) and Gordon Davies (Manchester City) had all moved on, most of them to more ambitious clubs than ourselves. We were left with a team of kids and, being the most experienced, I was made captain at the rookie age of 21. I'm not sure I was ready to lead others because I was still learning my trade, still gathering the experience I needed to fulfil my talent.

Rookie I may have been but at least I was no longer an apprentice because in those days juniors were given a torrid time by the professionals. It was not unusual to be cuffed around the head by them if you had done something wrong, like not cleaning their boots properly or leaving the dressing room in a mess. They enjoyed, like school prefects, the sadistic pleasure of being able to tell us what to do. They had a go at me for my colour, my sloppiness and anything else they could find to humiliate me, but in fairness they did the same to us all and in many ways it was a rite of passage.

Tony Gale nicknamed me "Arnie" from the television programme *Diff'rent Strokes* and Ray Houghton still calls me that. Everyone had to have a nickname. In fact only my mum calls me Paul, everyone else knows me as "Parks".

The deepest humiliation came at Christmas when all the apprentices were obliged to go into the dressing room, strip off and then stand on a bench in front of all the senior players one by one and sing a song. To 'help' us we were given props, namely the Wellington boots of groundsman Tom and a broom so that we could pretend to be playing a guitar. Then we had string attached to our penises, which our audience were not slow to pull, and there were buckets of cold water ready to be thrown at us if our performances were considered to be poor. It didn't help that I am the only black man born without rhythm so I don't think I covered myself with glory.

So petrified was Coney by the prospect of performing that he hid in the toilet of the Riverside Stand until it was all over. I can see now people like Lock, Strong and Gale laughing their heads off at us but they were only putting us in our lowly place and there was no malice intended. You dare not show any fear or, God forbid, cry because that would have only made things worse but, looking back, I don't think it did us any harm.

I doubt that it could happen now, I blame the YTS system for that because the players were not the club's but it made us mentally stronger. One of our problems, and it will catch up with us eventually, is that the young players today are not as mentally or physically as strong. There is no smacking at home and kids cannot contemplate leaving home because it is too costly until such time as they get a proper wage. Society strikes me as being softer, so, therefore, are our young footballers.

There were compensations to be had as apprentices. After a day of painting everything that did not move, washing kit in the machines and a multitude of other chores, we would stop for a drink at the Crabtree in Hammersmith or the

Eight Bells at Putney on our way home and we enjoyed each other's company.

In 1984/85 we were one point from the First Division. A year later we were relegated to the third. Perhaps I should have followed the others out of Craven Cottage to somewhere where I could carry on learning rather than to be a teacher to a gaggle of lads even younger than me. But I loved Fulham. I had lived and breathed the club for ten years from the age of 11 and I owed them everything. I was also a little unsure about where I should go next, or if I should go at all. I was assured things would improve and, crucially, I was loyal to Ray Harford. I did not want to let him down during a crisis, not a man who had done so much for me – and I did my best to steady a rapidly sinking ship.

I played in two more Under-21 internationals, against Turkey at Bristol in October and against Denmark at Manchester City in March, and always the dressing room talk was of money. I was one of very few players from outside the top flight and my £80 a week wages were dwarfed by those of my team-mates. Some of them earned three times as much, as I am sure they were quick to tell me. As Fulham plunged headlong towards the Third Division, it became clear I had to get out, but how I should leave and where I should go were altogether more complex questions.

My mind was made up when Harford left. Now there was no reason to stay. Les Strong, our stalwart left-back, was briefly caretaker and then Ray Lewington, an old friend and playing colleague, came in. Ray knew the club were struggling on the pitch and off it where there was no money to bring in reinforcements or to pay even the most basic bills. Dean Coney, a contemporary from our schooldays, was the club's other big asset and was also a member of the England Under-21 side. Coney and I went to see Lewington soon after his appointment, as I figured he must have suspected we might, and told him we needed to move on.

Ray was distraught. He did his best to keep us but I think deep down he knew he could not reasonably expect us to stay. My departure, however, was delayed for a whole, largely wasted year. The reason was my first major injury, a constantly 'popping' shoulder. I first dislocated the shoulder as a 14-year-old playing for Fulham's juniors against Ipswich, a match watched ironically by the Ipswich manager, Bobby Robson. For those who have never dislocated their shoulder, it is extremely painful and, once done, it can happen again and again. So it was with me. I even pulled it out of its socket hanging on to the dog as it ran towards the road on the end of its lead. After the eighth occasion it had become a real problem and on Live Aid Day in 1985 at the Wellington Hospital, London, I had the loose ligaments tied in knots in a bid to strengthen the flesh around the joint. I am pleased to say the operation was a complete success and I never did it again. But there is a life-long legacy. In cold weather there is still a noticeable ache.

So there I was at the start of the 1986/87 season, an England Under-21 international in the prime of his career at 22 and about to start my first season in the Third Division. Where my England Under-21 team-mates could look forward to matches at Old Trafford, Highbury and other grand arenas, my fixture list included Chesterfield and Chester. Not that I will hear a word said about such clubs because it was against them that I scored my first league goals. The record books say I got on the score-sheet in a 2-2 draw at Chester in September and the other in a 3-1 win over Chesterfield at Craven Cottage but I can't remember much about either, not even the manner of them and they were the first of not very many.

Over 15 or 16 years in professional football I only ever got a handful so when Manchester United eventually came to pay £1.8m for me it was certainly not for my prowess in front of opponents' goals. I don't know why this should be, but whenever I went into the opposition box for corners and free kicks, I never believed I would score. Yet when we were defending similar situations I won more than my share in the air and was usually in the right place on the ground when it came to making clearances. So it had to be a psychological block of sorts.

In any case, most of my managers never wanted me to go forward for set pieces. Being small and pacy and a good reader of developing moves, I was encouraged to hang back on the halfway line to block counter attacks while bigger defenders were sent to danger areas. It was the same for Des Walker who got even fewer than me over a longer career.

My problem was that I was trapped by a contract I came to regret signing in the 'glory' era of the Second Division under Macdonald and in those days, without agents to provoke moves, you often had to sit them out. I knew I was stagnating and so did Coney but until such time as some other club came in for us we had to carry on at Craven Cottage, our tolerance and loyalty tested every week. There is no getting away from the fact that we had a bad side even by Third Division standards, full of youngsters who had served no real kind of apprenticeship and other players on the way down. Our dwindling number of fans must have thought we would at least be a power in the Third Division. But they were wrong. We finished 18th and avoided another relegation by a whisker. Strangled by a lack of money, the club was in free-fall and it was not until Mohamed Al-Fayed took over that the decline was finally halted.

It all came to a head at Liverpool in the League Cup. Two years previously against the same opposition I had announced myself as an emerging talent. This time I was part of a youthful side slaughtered 10-0. The pitch at Anfield had been watered and it was among the most humiliating and embarrassing moments of my life. If it had not been for our goalkeeper, John Vaughan, it is no exaggeration to say it could have been 20 such was our complete annihilation.

Coney and I hated every minute as incessant red waves engulfed us.

Everyone who knows me will tell you that I rarely lose my temper and being a mere 5ft 7ins, never get involved in fights. But at the height of our misery I tore into young Brian Cottington, accusing him of bottling a challenge. Brian answered back and it needed the timely intervention of Alan Hansen to prevent a fracas breaking out. I was so frustrated and so furious and I have never been so glad to hear a final whistle. As we trooped dejectedly off the pitch, I realised that my Fulham days were over. The next time I came to Anfield I wanted it to be on an equal footing.

Not that life was much easier in the league. We suffered a club record home league defeat by Port Vale, being hammered 6-0 with Andy Jones scoring five of them, and I think we were lucky to stay up. My own performances were affected inevitably so that I began to think that I might never get away but there was still a residual loyalty to Fulham and I hated tales of our financial plight. Our chairman, David Bulstrode, got more headlines than the team when he proposed a merger with Queens Park Rangers, a prospect which infuriated those supporters who were still loyal to our cause.

At our lowest point, Jimmy Hill, a big television name at the time and a former Fulham playing hero in the 1950s, came in at the head of a consortium to buy his old club. Hill could see the financial chaos threatening to engulf us and wanted to do what he could. Hill had a reputation as a bit of a self-publicist but I think he genuinely cared about Fulham and felt that he, above all others, stood a good chance of saving us. Eventually he became chairman and, in a typically flamboyant gesture, Hill invited the whole playing staff to the house he owned in Brighton.

Here he had a mini-golf range and he invited us all to hit balls into the netting at the end of his garden. At the same time he spoke to every member of the staff except me, the club captain. I don't know why he was so rude, but he was. I can only guess that he thought it pointless because I was about to be sold. If I was, I did not know about it. In a fit of pique, I drove a golf ball the other way through his patio window. What I did not realise was that Bulstrode was about to depart for Queens Park Rangers as their chairman in place of Jim Gregory and I think something must have been happening behind the scenes.

Soon afterwards, at the end of a thoroughly miserable season, Coney and I were told we were being sold to Queens Park Rangers at a combined fee of £425,000. We were the last of the Fulham crown jewels to depart and we were not given much chance to say no. At least we were joining a club, upwardly mobile and, for me, a shy Essex lad, just down the road. For Coney and I it was a wonderful opportunity because we were still handcuffed to a Fulham contract. There was more money and better opportunities and I subsequently learned from a Fulham director, Dave Gardner, that the money received from the transfer saved the club from going under.

My last appearance for Fulham was a midday May Bank Holiday match with Harry Redknapp's Bournemouth at Craven Cottage. Tony Sealy, an ex-Fulham player, got one of their goals in a 3-1 defeat which gave them the championship and with most of the 9,000 crowd up from the south coast, it was a low, low point. I was glad to be going.

To this day I retain a strong affection for the Cottagers. I look for their results and I follow their progress. I am pleased also that Al-Fayed came in and began to restore them to former glories. As a youngster I had been fed on tales of Johnny Haynes and other heroes and knew, that by repute, they should have been a big club. They were when I joined but they were not when I headed off to Loftus Road, ready to make a fresh start and eager to make up for lost time.

Chapter 4

Progress on the plastic

PETER SHREEVES was Jim Smith's assistant manager when I arrived at Queens Park Rangers in June 1987 and he told me exactly what he thought of me on day one. "You are a good defender," he said. "You can head, tackle and recover. But you can't f***ing pass the ball. Give it to someone who can." Welcome to Loftus Road, I remember thinking.

That comment, honestly given and a fair appraisal, hurt my pride, but it was the truth in one brutal sentence. I had coasted at Fulham perhaps for a year, maybe even two, and had got into a nice comfortable rut. As the club declined on and off the pitch I ceased caring and, as a result, did myself an injustice. I resented being at Craven Cottage and my own performances suffered badly. A good manager had been sacked, my mentor Ray Harford had gone and only the presence of Dean Coney kept me sane. At least we were in this mess together.

At one stage, before QPR came in, I really believed I might be at Fulham for the rest of my football life. I had resigned myself to that prospect, so I have to thank Jim Smith and Peter Shreeves for rescuing me. Another year at Fulham and I might well have gone backwards even further. But here I was at Queens Park Rangers and here was the assistant manager saying I couldn't pass. No one at Fulham would have dared say such a thing because I was too important to upset.

What price loyalty, in any case? The one-club man of old is a dying breed because it is not in the interests of players or their agents to stay as Johnny Haynes had done, for instance, at Fulham all his career. We should, also as an example, be praising Matthew Le Tissier as one of the great British players of his generation with a host of caps and medals to prove it. Instead he is a legend only in his own small pond because he never left the comfort zone of Southampton. Who knows what he might have achieved had he been persuaded to join a big club and tested himself week in, week out? Football is about winning trophies, open-topped buses, pressure matches in foreign parts.

I believe Le Tissier was unambitious not to leave Southampton; he could have always gone back. Had he gone to a big club, as I did later to Manchester United, his whole life would have been transformed. When I went to Old Trafford, my entire mentality was changed overnight. There were people to help with my diet, my psychological approach, everything. That is because at clubs like Manchester United, every match is a cup final, everyone wants to beat you and the demand for success is incredible. You either wilt under that sort of pressure or you thrive on it.

My experience at Loftus Road enabled me to cope. But we all want to win major competitions and play for our country, that's why we come into football. I could have stayed at Fulham and I could have stayed at QPR but I wanted to play for a big club in big matches every week. I had that desire. Fans sometimes struggle to understand that because 99 per cent of them have it and they just don't get it when a professional player doesn't. At United, as I was later to discover, you had to give 100 per cent in every match and play with injuries where necessary. Luckily for me I saw little point in not fully exploiting my ability, even if I could not pass the ball to the satisfaction of some.

Rangers were assembling a powerful and attractive side and had, as an additional ally, their infamous plastic pitch. Jim Smith was the first manager I ever called "gaffer" or "boss", which I suppose said something about the easy and sheltered regimes at Fulham. Smith was your archetypal blunt Yorkshireman and was as volatile as any manager I ever came across – until I met Alex Ferguson. Smith had an authority about him which demanded our respect and was not afraid to use his own 'hair-dryer' treatment when the need arose. He expected us to work hard on the pitch and in training. If you did that, he would be happy, but he was the first manager I knew who would stop practice sessions to issue a rollicking if he felt players were slacking. Straight away, I knew I was going to have to work harder because the players around me were so much better and because that is what the manager made it clear he wanted.

Four years previously Rangers had taken the mickey out of my Fulham in beating us 3-1 on the Loftus Road plastic pitch and it's true that many opponents were suspicious of it and were sometimes as good as beaten before the kick-off. But it made my two-division jump all the easier because it was a surface made for my type of game. Jim had spent about £1m on new players and there was some tremendous quality in the side with people like David Seaman, Alan McDonald, Terry Fenwick and Gary Bannister, while the surface made for the slick passing for which we became renowned.

My job was to man-mark and I soon came to realise that with my speed, if the ball was ever played over me, on the plastic pitch it would run away. No one would catch it. So, armed with that knowledge I could enjoy some comfortable afternoons while opposing strikers ran themselves into the ground trying to catch the ball as it ran through, inevitably, to big David Seaman. Much as I enjoyed playing on it and much as it aided our style, there were down sides. My legs were like lead on a Sunday and Monday and my muscles felt like they had been hit by sticks. If we had a home game on the following Tuesday, it was hard to be fully fit or to feel in proper shape. There are also permanent reminders of the infamous plastic in the shape of scars on my elbow, thigh and knee. The 'burn' marks were painful and were never given the chance to heal because we played so many matches on it. I ruined many a good pair of trousers on a Saturday night out because the weeping wound would stick to the material like glue.

I made my competitive debut at Upton Park, of all places, and my job was to man-mark Tony Cottee, who was just beginning to show the sort of form that would make him a Hammers legend. We won 3-0 and Cottee was taken off, my job done. Bearing in mind what West Ham had come to symbolise for me, I am pleased to say I went through my career without ever losing there. It was a good season overall, and we even led the table in August when Smith was Manager of the Month.

I began to make up ground again after my two lost years at Fulham and I got rave reviews for my marking of Graeme Sharp, Paul Walsh and then Wayne Clarke of Everton when we beat the champions 1-0 at Loftus Road. Martin Allen scored the winner. What surprised many people who had not seen me at this level was my ability to out-jump people much taller than myself. As I was saying, it was a natural talent but my ability to nullify expensive individual threats led to frustration among opponents.

Never more was this evident than at Newcastle where I came across the mercurial Paul Gascoigne for the first time. I was allowing a ball to run out of play for a goal kick for about the hundredth time that afternoon when I suddenly felt a succession of blows being aimed at the back of my neck. Only Gazza could have thought he would get away with that. A furious, red-faced and protesting Gazza was duly sent off while I said nothing. It was never part of my character to get involved or react to an incident like that and in any case there was never any doubt of the identity of the culprit.

The dressing room at Loftus Road was full of big characters and was the most disturbing and volatile of my career, and that includes Old Trafford. Professional football is a bitchy game and you have to remember you are not necessarily playing with your mates as you might on a Sunday morning. It could get nasty in there and the secret of surviving this jungle was not to make yourself an easy target. Unfortunately it did not take much to attract attention. You only had to mispronounce or say the wrong word and the others feasted on your mistake. Enter the room also with a strange-looking shirt, socks or underpants and you would be a target for the rest of the day for the wit of Ray Wilkins, Dave Bardsley, Terry Fenwick or Alan McDonald. Under no circumstances must you bite back or sulk or look offended. That only made it worse and the stick would only grow more intense. I can only imagine the atmosphere was like a women's dressing room at a fashion show, sharp-tongued, occasionally bitter and, once or twice, a little hostile.

Bardsley, McDonald and Mark Dennis could be disgusting to each other and, until he adapted, Wilkins admitted he did not know what he had walked into when he joined us. Central defender Danny Maddix was the butt of most jokes and Bardsley's cutting comments and would sometimes over-react, but I have to say, despite the bitchiness, there was no real malice and team spirit was good. Even now, after years out of the game, the dressing room banter is the part of the game I miss most and other ex-pros constantly say the same. When I play in tournaments now with other former players it's great to hear the crack and the wit, but once that's over I'm just as happy to be out of it and home, as I was back then. In a strange sort of way, the fear of being a victim made me a better player. The last thing I wanted was to be known in the dressing room for my poor passing or to be criticised on the pitch for not doing my job properly, so my technique improved dramatically.

Wilkins, meanwhile, became something of an initiator, out of self-preservation perhaps, of the dressing room japes and jokes (yes, that is the same Ray Wilkins that always seems so calm and in control and just a little bit dull when you see him on TV).

Terry Fenwick was an interesting character. In many ways I found Fenwick to be a clone of his mentor, Terry Venables. He was bright, studious and possessed a good brain but you never knew what he was thinking. Fenwick, who gave good service later to Tottenham and England, was a great sweeper behind McDonald and I and he was a canny operator. I remember once being drawn in to marking an opponent who was not the man I was supposed to be looking after. I shouted to Terry to watch my back and seconds later there lay my opponent in a big heap on the ground, injured. Terry was nowhere to be seen, but we all knew what had happened. Terry had indeed done a good job.

I had a lot of time for McDonald, our big blond centre-half. I rated him every bit as highly as Steve Bruce who performed such heroics for Manchester United when I was there. He came over from Northern Ireland to West London in search of a career and it must have been a big upheaval for a young lad but Rangers became his club and he wore the blue and white hoops with true pride.

My admiration for Bruce is just as great because he served a hard apprenticeship through the lower divisions. I played against him for Fulham when he was at his first club, Gillingham, and my initial encounter with him ended with me being pushed by him into the stands at Priestfield. He was obviously determined to win and winning was very important to all players in those days.

63

Simply put – at Fulham and Queens Park Rangers I needed to play and I needed to win to make any kind of money. I reckon 35 per cent of my salary was made up of a win bonus and another 25 per cent came from an appearance bonus. I had a Ford Capri and I never knew whether or not I would be able, from week to week, to pay the instalments on it. I feared a bad run or being out of the team because the fate of my beloved Capri was at stake. Now players get their money win, lose or draw, such incentives long gone in terms of a major percentage of their income.

When I first joined QPR, we were a match for any side, not least Manchester United. We may have had a smaller stadium and our plastic pitch but we could look any of the teams regarded as major today firmly in the eye. United beat us at Loftus Road in my first season but then in the return at Old Trafford on 30th April, I got on the score-sheet – for United. Bruce gave United the lead but McDonald equalised and with seven minutes to go it looked as if we might get a deserved draw. Then Bryan Robson knocked a long ball into our area and I chased after it, fractionally ahead of Peter Davenport, the United striker. Davenport was McDonald's man so I had cut across to snuff out the danger. But as Seaman came off his line, I met the ball on the volley and my intended back-pass looped over him into the net. It was a sort of paintbrush touch, off my laces, but strong enough to fly over David and yet weak enough to dip under the bar and all our good work was destroyed with one simple error. Who said my passing was inaccurate?

So we finished fifth and in most other years that position would have been enough to guarantee European competition the following season but in the wake of the Heysel disaster where so many spectators were killed, English clubs were still banned and our achievements had no reward or outlet.

My own reward for a good season was to be selected for my first England B international in Malta and here I came across Graham Taylor, the B team manager, for the first time. We stayed in a Fawlty Towers type of hotel and I came on as a substitute for Chris Fairclough. It was also the first time I played alongside Steve Bruce. I can honestly say that at that stage of my career I had no thoughts of playing for England. Daydreams, yes, but no genuine belief that I might one day represent my country at the highest level. I might be accused of lacking ambition here but there were so many good, established players around that I just never thought I was in the queue, let alone at the front of it. I saw the B cap as nothing more than recognition that I was now in the First Division and doing well.

Rangers fans also recognised my worth by naming me Player of the Year, as they did the following season. We slipped to ninth in 1988/89 and it was a more turbulent year than my first with the chairman David Bulstrode dying, Jim Smith departing to Newcastle in an attempt to revive the ultimate in football's sleeping giants and then Peter Shreeves and Trevor Francis taking over at the helm in quick succession. Bulstrode had been instrumental in my joining QPR but he had been good to me and Coney at Fulham before he, too, left the club and became Rangers' chairman. All the while Bulstrode was at Fulham I had been content to stay and I was glad to be moving with him, so to speak, to another part of West London and glad that he would be in control. When he died of a heart attack at his home in Jersey, I was devastated for he had been a good friend and had genuinely cared about my welfare.

Richard Thompson replaced him as chairman, a keen Arsenal fan in his 20s whom we nicknamed Pinocchio, not because he told lies or had a long nose but because he looked so young. He spent a lot of money on people like Peter Reid, Mark Stein and Andy Sinton but it was a bad blow when Smith gave way to his ambition to manage a really big club. Smith gave me my opportunity at Loftus Road and my first reaction was to follow him to Newcastle if that had been possible. Sadly it was not, but I am not sure he got what he had hoped for at St James' Park and later that season he suffered the ignominy of losing to us there. Everyone liked the idea of the quick-witted Peter Shreeves as caretaker. It was a popular decision but, as I had discovered at Fulham, popular decisions about caretakers becoming managers were not necessarily the right ones.

So it was perhaps for the best that Trevor Francis was appointed player-manager three months later in December 1988. Trevor was a great England footballer of 52 caps, still an excellent player in the First Division as he approached the veteran stage and everything about him was thoroughly professional. But Trevor, a teenage prodigy at Birmingham, could also be stubborn and his main concern was always transparently himself. I got on well with him and still do but there were others who set out to make his life difficult. I am sorry that there were those also who tried to take liberties with him and, for their own gain, did not give him the respect his record in the game had demanded.

The problem, I think, was that he made himself unpopular with the players by setting such high standards. Trevor would be quick to criticise and, like many great natural players, could not understand that there were those who did not share his ability or could respond in the way he expected. He used to berate injury victims, yet was himself quick to stand down if he was in any way unfit. He was an awesome player but hard to please off the pitch.

One player who damaged him was Martin Allen, a hard-tackling midfielder, who was not known as "Mad Dog" for nothing. We were playing at Newcastle and staying close by on the Friday night when Allen decided he wanted to go back to London to be with his wife who was close to giving birth. Allen booked out of the hotel at 6am, swearing his room-mate Justin Channing to secrecy. It was not until lunchtime, three hours before kick-off, that we realised Allen had gone, leaving us to fill the gap an apprentice.

There were no birth complications or other problems and Trevor took a huge amount of criticism for not showing enough compassion but I felt sorry for him. Newspaper and magazine columnists went to town on "uncaring" Francis but the fault was all Allen's. Allen was fined two weeks' wages, which led to Francis losing the respect of some of the players for coming down so heavily against him. The whole situation became a bit of a mess, but it was all of Allen's making. I notice Allen is now forging a reputation for his eccentric style of management and I wish him well but I found him to be selfish and self-righteous and one of the most unpleasant people I ever met in football. He was always stirring behind the scenes. I was disappointed Seaman used to spend so much of his time with Allen and was influenced by him.

We all remember Gazza's tears at Italia 90 but at this point in my career all I knew about him was that he tried to punch his way through the back of my head that day at St James' Park. I came across him again as a team-mate in a bizarre experience when we went to Reykjavik for a B international against Iceland – an aptly named country if ever there was one.

We flew from Scotland for the match at the tail-end of the 1988/89 season. The World Cup was little more than a year away and Bobby Robson wanted to look at some fringe candidates for his squad, people like me, Gazza, David Platt, David Beasant, Tony Dorigo, Gary Pallister, Gary Mabbutt and Terry Hurlock. There were two things I will always remember from that match, the bitter cold and the National Front presence among England's travelling support. Even in the middle of May there was freezing rain. Paul Stewart and Dorigo had to come off suffering from hypothermia. They needed cold showers to warm up again but it was the abuse I received from the National Front which made my blood freeze. Why these people had come all the way to Iceland I will never understand.

They gave Gazza some stick for being too fat but that was genial enough. In my case it was non-stop anti-black and, as I was the only non-white in the team, it was as if they had travelled for the specific purpose of abusing me, such was its intensity and persistence. There was nothing anyone could do for me. I just had to take it and get on with the business of playing, pretending it had nothing to do with me. Luckily I had learned from an early age to ignore all racist taunts and at least I was able to run around to keep warm. The so-called England supporters froze in the rain and it was hard to sympathise with them.

Hurlock and Steve Bull got our goals in a 2-0 win. Bull became something of a cult hero among England fans during that season and we were always surprised with the amount of fan mail he received every day in the post. His career at Wolves had begun in the lower divisions, but he had always scored goals, no matter what level he had played at and it seemed to be the same now he was making the step up to international level. His goal sparked a frenzy in the contingent of travelling fans. We played pretty well and were good value for the win.

But the excitement that night was by no means over. We went into Reykjavik for a few drinks and we discovered the locals had a curious way of enjoying themselves. Whenever they had finished their beer they threw the containers over their shoulders on to the ground so that the floor of the pub was covered in glass and broken bottles. We had to pick our way through the debris to get out and even then the fun had not finished. As we piled into the back of a taxi, a drinker from the pub we had just left, obviously the worse for wear, clambered in alongside us. Bull told him to get out but he refused, saying he had got in first. Bull asked him again, and once more he refused.

What happened then can only be described as Black Country justice. Sufficient to say, Bull persuaded him to leave one way or another and bundled him out of the cab on to the pavement. I liked Bull. He was an aggressive, powerful player but his loyalty to Wolves, as admirable as Le Tissier's was to Southampton in its way, meant that we never knew how good he was or could have been as he never played top flight football, despite being a success for a time at international level.

For all my diffidence and a certain lack of confidence that stemmed from my humble football background, Bobby Robson had followed my progress from the day he saw me nursing a dislocated shoulder playing against Ipswich's youth team and watched me develop to the extent that he identified me as having England potential. Some of the newspapers started tipping me as an international candidate even if I had not recognised it in myself at this stage. I was called into the full squad as part of the learning process, Robson making it very clear that it was extremely unlikely that I would be capped at least for a game or two and only then if my club form continued to be of a high standard.

So it was a case of watching, listening and being patient until I finally got my chance in a World Cup qualifier on April 26th 1989 against Albania. I had just turned 25 and was absolutely elated and still in awe of those other members of the England squad; Bryan Robson, Terry Butcher, Peter Shilton, Gary Lineker. I may have played against them at club level but it was another step altogether training and playing with household names. Wembley was always a wonderful sight for internationals and there were more than 60,000 there to see us win 4-0 on our way to qualification for Italia 90.

Bobby was a meticulous man who insisted that we serve a kind of England apprenticeship and he expected us to show the same level of patriotism and pride in our country. Englishmen are sometimes noted for being a little reticent in showing their national fervour, but not Bobby. It was like a religion to him. He had played for England and now he was the manager and, as far as he was concerned, there could be no higher honour. That is one of the reasons Bobby made us wait for our international chance. He wanted it to be a career pinnacle to play for England and I am not sure it means quite the same now. I don't think it is necessarily the privilege it should be to represent your country. In my opinion caps are handed out much more easily than they used to be, partly because there are fewer players of international quality so the competition is not so great, and, as a result, being capped by England does not merit the respect it once did.

In the present era, players called into the England squad for the first time are being capped straight away, there is no nervous wait and, I dare say, not nearly the same sense of achievement. I suggest caps are only handed out for competitive matches or if a player has been on the pitch for more than 30 minutes. Think today how many players are being capped for coming on in the last minute as a substitute and sometimes not even touching the ball before the final whistle. I can think of several examples of players in the last decade who certainly wouldn't have amassed anything like the number of caps that they have if this rule of thumb had been in operation.

Had I received caps for every time I was in an England squad I would have earned many more than my 19. I might also have had one less if caps were issued only, as I suggest, for those on the pitch for 30 minutes because my debut lasted 13 of normal time and a little more for injuries. Officially I came on in the 77th minute for Gary Stevens of Everton by which time the match was already over as a contest. The team that night was Shilton, Stevens, Pearce, Webb, Walker, Butcher, Robson, Rocastle, Beardsley, Lineker and Waddle. Gazza replaced Rocastle ten minutes before I came on. Mine was a gentle start at right-back, a position foreign to me at Queens Park Rangers where I was a centre-half or sweeper, but at least I had started and I was as proud, the black son of a Jamaican, as any Englishman could be.

Robson kept faith with me by naming me in the squad for the summer internationals which included more World Cup qualifiers and friendlies against Chile and Denmark, but before then there was serious drinking to be done. Magaluf has a reputation as a footballer's watering hole and that is where I could be found three days before my full debut against Chile, completely drunk.

One of my best friends is Tommy South, who later developed Purfleet Football Club into a decent non-league side from humble county league beginnings. Tommy suggested a group of us spend three days in the resort and who was I to disagree. For 72 hours we drank and drank and drank. We spent most of our time in a bar called Mano's where I ended up serving customers from behind the bar while wearing a mask of the Queen. Bobby Robson liked us to be patriotic but this was probably going too far.

One of the Spanish waiters kept a duck which he used to bring into the pub and put it up the skirts and the shirts of the inebriated as a surprise. One day the laugh was on him. A drinker took exception to the duck and broke its neck. Three days later I was walking out at Wembley to take on Chile for my first England start. Had Robson known what I had been doing in Magaluf, I think my international career would have stalled.

I was right-back again in a back four of me, Walker, Butcher and Pearce. An experimental partnership of Nigel Clough and John Fashanu were up front in a goalless draw. I didn't play in the 3-0 win over Poland in the final qualifier of the season or in our demolition of the Scots at Hampden Park in which Steve Bull scored on his full debut. But I did start again against Denmark on 7th June. Lineker scored our goal in a 1-1 draw and I went in to the summer break a fully-fledged England international, three times capped and with the prospect of the World Cup a year away.

To be sure of a place in the England team I needed a good domestic season in 1989/90 and I got it. I was Rangers' Player of the Year for the third time and in many respects I was approaching the peak of my career. In December I was named captain, succeeding Peter Reid who had moved on to Manchester City, and I came to love leading the club on the pitch. I had developed a great affection for Rangers and I think it was fair to say it was my best season at Loftus Road. We reached the FA Cup quarter-finals beating Arsenal on the way and some of our football was a joy for spectators and players alike. However I was always aware that my wages of about £600 or £700 a week did not compare favourably with those of my England contemporaries, some of whom were earning two or three times as much. On one international trip around this time, Bryan Robson casually mentioned that Alex Ferguson rated me highly if I was ever thinking of leaving QPR. There was nothing more to it than that and I laughed it off. I was in love with Queens Park Rangers and had no desire or thought of moving.

During the summer of 1989, Don Howe left Wimbledon to become assistant to Trevor Francis and I am glad he did because I think he had a big influence on me getting into the England squad for the 1990 World Cup. Don was also number two to Bobby Robson in the England hierarchy so I was aware of him before he came to Rangers. In his playing prime Don had appeared for West Bromwich Albion, Arsenal and England as a full-back. Kenny Sansom, the former Arsenal and England player, who by now had joined us at Rangers, knew him from his time at Highbury and did a wicked impersonation.

Don was no youngster, but his enthusiasm was incredible. Not for him standing on the sidelines. Don wanted to be involved in every session, showing us physically exactly what he required of us and getting us worried because in the heat he would pant and puff to the point of exhaustion bearing in mind he had only recently undergone a heart by-pass operation. The Hoops were on the up. Luton's Roy Wegerle became our first £1m signing, Bardsley and Sansom had also arrived and player-manager Francis showed glimpses of his rare talent in scoring a hat-trick against Aston Villa in September.

But two months later our world was rocked when Francis quit and Howe was elevated to the position of chief coach, something of a novelty in those days. There were, thankfully, enough good players to see us through this little crisis and it was a happy season until I became involved in an incident which came close to costing me my place in the World Cup squad.

Looking back I realise how lucky I was that I had Bobby Robson and Don Howe fighting my corner. And it was all because I was sent off for the first time in my career in a meaningless match with Manchester City in April 1990 for retaliation just as Robson prepared to name his squad to travel to Italy. A team-mate and good friend, Simon Barker, had his leg broken in a clash with Paul Lake and tempers became frayed. Gary Megson flicked my ankles and we both went down. As we rose I kneed him in the face right in front of the referee, Jeff Winter. Why I did it, I don't know because I had hardly ever been booked before, but I did not even wait for Winter to raise his red card. I fled to the dressing room, little realising that my ordeal was just about to start.

I was of course suspended for three matches, the standard tariff for a dismissal for violent conduct. But there were only two remaining of that season and since I had broken a toe in the City match I would not have played again anyway. That was the good part. The problem was that I was technically suspended until after the first domestic match of the following season. During my suspension I was left out of the international with Czechoslovakia and I came to realise there were certain members of the FA's gin and tonic brigade who were against me going to the World Cup on the basis that I was still banned.

At the time there existed an unwritten rule that players undergoing domestic suspensions would not be selected for England duty. Nowadays it would not have provoked such a crisis but it was a big talking point at the time and I feared for my place. I felt the FA had not taken my previously good disciplinary record into account and it needed Robson to stand up for me and insist they relent. Had he not done so, I think the closest I would have got to Italia 90 was watching it on television.

Chapter 5

The magic of the World Cup

W HEN ENGLAND were preparing for the epic adventure of the World Cup in Italy in 1990, I shared a room at our hotel in Burnham Beeches, Buckinghamshire, with David Rocastle, the Arsenal midfield player. We were among 26 players keeping fit and getting ready in the knowledge that four of us would be culled before we set off because only 22 were allowed in the final party. So it was also a nervous time for us all, wondering which of us would be told by Bobby Robson, our manager, to go home because we were not going to be needed.

My brush with the FA establishment over my suspension, while worrying, also, oddly, gave me peace of mind because Robson had fought behind the scenes for my inclusion in the party. Had I not been in his plans I don't think he would have bothered. But there was no getting away from the fact that I was still on the fringes and relatively inexperienced at international level so I could assume nothing.

While I drank beer, David preferred brandy and Babycham, a real black person's drink (something a bit sweet), and every night he was on the phone to say goodnight to his little daughter Melissa. We got on well and enjoyed each other's company among a strong group of seasoned professionals, many of whom had already made a mark for England and who represented a formidable group of players, arguably the best since we won the World Cup in 1966.

The 26 comprised Peter Shilton (Derby), Chris Woods (Rangers), David Seaman (Arsenal), Dave Beasant (Chelsea), Gary Stevens (Rangers), Stuart Pearce (Forest), Des Walker (Forest), Terry Butcher (Rangers), Paul Parker (QPR), Mark Wright (Derby), Tony Adams (Arsenal), Tony Dorigo (Chelsea), Neil Webb (Manchester United), Bryan Robson (Manchester United), Steve McMahon (Liverpool), David Platt (Aston Villa), Steve Hodge (Forest), Paul Gascoigne (Spurs), Trevor Steven (Rangers), David Rocastle (Arsenal), Chris Waddle (Marseille), John Barnes (Liverpool), Peter Beardsley (Liverpool), Gary Lineker (Spurs), Steve Bull (Wolves), and Alan Smith (Arsenal).

Not many weaknesses there with Bull the only Third Division player and the squad solid in all departments. I fully expected to be sharing with "Rocky", as we knew him, for the next four and a half weeks. Then one day Robson knocked on our door and looking at me, beckoned me out with his thumb over his shoulder. He obviously wanted a word with Rocastle and I left without a word or a glance. Minutes later I went back in, Robson had long gone and there was Rocastle crying his eyes out, his World Cup dream all over in the space of one short, sharp 30-second conversation. My own eyes filled up. I could only guess what he was feeling. What should have been the pinnacle of his career, as it was to be for me, had been snatched away from him.

Dave did not want to hang about, understandably, and I helped him begin the task of packing his bags in preparation to make the disconsolate journey home. I helped him carry his cases to his car and loaded them into the boot. We must have looked like a gay couple as we hugged in the car park before we cleared our throats and became macho again but it was a defining moment of sorts, unquestionably my hardest moment in football. I was going to the World Cup, the game's biggest showpiece, and he was not. At least Melissa would get to see her daddy that night.

Dave Beasant, Tony Adams and Alan Smith were the others to miss out and Robson said later how difficult it was to make the choice and then tell the unlucky players they were not going to Italy. Adams came from Rainham, my neck of the woods, and was strong enough to bounce back to play many more times for England – although he did admit to a four-day drinking 'bender' after his omission – but I'm not sure Rocastle was ever quite the same player. After being a key figure in Arsenal's resurgence in winning the league twice and the League Cup around that time, he was sold to Leeds, then Manchester City, Chelsea and Norwich without being able to reproduce the great vitality of his Arsenal days. I think Robson believed that in Platt, Webb, Hodge and McMahon he had enough players to augment fixtures in the side like Bryan Robson, Waddle and Gascoigne. Someone had to miss out. Rocky's life ended in tragedy when he was diagnosed with lymphoma and died soon afterwards in March 2001, two months short of his 34th birthday.

Beasant has got to be one of the most fortunate players ever to be part of a World Cup squad and he can thank me for getting an unexpected late chance to take part in this trip of a lifetime. We were at our training camp in Sardinia and our manager decided to have an open day for the press and to allow our session to be watched by our many fans who had followed us out. It was supposed to be a public relations afternoon but it went horribly wrong for Seaman and me.

Sure enough, the invitation to let in the fans meant abuse for me and John Barnes as the two black players but we had learned not to let it affect us and got on with what we were told was going to be an easy session. The problem was that many of us took it too easily for Robson's liking and he stopped it to administer a rollicking, making the reasonable point that the press and a whole swathe of supporters would be getting the wrong impression of our preparations. Robson singled me out for special condemnation and I had a go back at him because I felt we were all a bit lackadaisical, not just me.

In a sort of fit of indignation I swung wildly at the next ball which came my way and I can say it now, I have never struck a shot as sweetly in my life. It flew at great speed towards Seaman who was not looking. The next thing we heard was a cry of pain from our goalkeeper and worried medical men were soon surrounding him with looks of concern. Verdict: one broken thumb. Culprit: a contrite Paul Parker. We needed a special sanction from Fifa to allow Seaman, whose World Cup was over, to be replaced by a reprieved and relieved Beasant.

Bobby Robson was notoriously forgetful about names and he used to call me Danny Thomas. Thomas was built like me and had a good career at Coventry and Tottenham and had he not already retired three years previously, he might even have been called into the World Cup squad by mistake. Bobby didn't mean it as an insult, he forgot the names of bigger and better players than me, it was all part of his eccentricity and extended to not remembering the name of the country we were playing or individual opponents. There were always prompters on hand.

If I could have hand-picked a club manager it would have been him, certainly until Alex Ferguson came along. At that stage he was the best I had come across. Both had this colossal appetite for the game and both had every quality you, as a player, would want in a manager although there was an element of Robson the good cop and Fergie the bad cop in their approach. Both also had this fantastic desire to win and if you had anything about you as a player it would be bound to improve you.

Robson was a lovely bloke and he had this capacity to get the best out of every player through building us up as individuals. His team talks were great orations of enthusiasm and while he gave everything of himself in those, he expected and got the same from his players. International players are no different from those at club level in that they need to know if the manager wants them. Are we in, or are we out? Some managers would avoid such issues but Robson would never lie and Ipswich players I met from his great days there always said they knew where they stood with him. As a result they worked hard for him, and so it was with us.

When he told me I was going to Italy, it felt like he was my dad even if he did call me Danny. One of Bobby's great platforms, the basis of many a team meeting on the eve of battle, was that opponents feared us because we were England. That always struck a chord with me and I think it did the rest of the squad. It made us feel proud and I know there was not a player in Italy that year who did not love and respect him. That was why I was amazed at the way Newcastle's players appeared to disrespect him in the build-up to his undignified exit at St James' Park. Did they not know what he had achieved as a player and as a manager? Much more than most of those will, I suspect.

Bobby's team talks were not to be missed but there was one occasion when I was late for one of his up-and-at-'em talks at Burnham Beeches. In those days I lived not 30 minutes away from the hotel at Wokingham and on the way back from a few hours at home I got caught in traffic. Bobby was in full flow when I eventually reached the hotel, so much so that I figured it might be best not to go into the room where he was giving an impassioned speech to the rest of the squad. Don Howe spotted me and indicated by signs that I should somehow creep in on my hands and knees. This was of course an open invitation for all the others to kick me on my silent path to a vacant chair at the back of the room. Just as I managed to slide on to it, Bobby said: "Can you hear me at the back?" To which I replied: "Perfectly thanks." I thought I had got away with it, but Howe later gave me a roasting and I had no complaints.

That aside, there was a good spirit among the players as we left for our training camp in Sardinia and much of that was to Bobby's credit. Bobby wanted happy players and while he would not tolerate fools, sulkers or mickey-takers, he backed us all and we all backed him. It was a mutually agreeable relationship. He was strong when he spoke, never swore and I was lucky in many ways because, as a man of great sentiment, he had very strong feelings for Fulham, his and my first club, often telling me how as a 16-year-old he had headed to London from his home in the north-east to start his football career. It must have taken great courage to have left all he knew so young but as a result I think he liked me, whatever name he called me.

Bobby always marvelled at my ability to jump so high and wondered if I had inherited such a skill from my parents. Purely as an aside, my parents never saw me play professionally and for that I am grateful because I would have been concerned about them in a football-watching environment. My brothers did and I know they were proud but sister Doreen stayed away in case there was crowd criticism of me. She would have remonstrated with my critics.

Bobby's problem was that he had got off to a bad start before a ball had been kicked. After talks over a new contract with the Football Association, his employers, had broken down, he announced that once the finals were over he would be going to manage the crack Dutch side, PSV Eindhoven. This did not go down at all well with the press or public. Not many years previously, Don Revie had walked out of the England manager's job, the country's top appointment, and had fled to the Middle East to fill his boots with gold (and sand). Some of the criticism of Robson was a bit hysterical, along the lines that he was deserting his country in the hour of need and that his mind would inevitably be elsewhere as the competition was unfolding. As a result, there was an air of tension between him and the press and there was a danger of a siege mentality developing.

Gary Stevens was the man in front of me in Robson's pecking order of full-backs. What was in my favour was that I could play at right-back, as a central defender or sweeper, but I wondered if I would get any chance to play when we left Sardinia to play in our final warm-up friendly in Tunisia on 2nd June. Robson was loyal to those who had served him well and Stevens had done that. The wives, who had accompanied us to Sardinia, went home and we swapped a glorious hotel for a much poorer one in Tunisia which I found to be an awful place and I was a spectator to an awful match, drawn 1-1.

Any complacency we had as a team was shattered but it did not stop the press criticising us and I suppose we deserved it. It was also at a time when a woman revealed an affair with our manager in a tabloid newspaper and while it must have embarrassed him, he did not show it. There was a by-product. We always had the English papers at our hotel, partly to see what the reporters were saying about us but also to keep in touch with what was going on at home. These were now banned.

Had we beaten the Republic of Ireland in the opening World Cup group match I might never have kicked a ball in the tournament. As it was, we scrambled a 1-1 draw which I watched from the bench. The Irish side was full of players we met every week in the English First Division and the teams cancelled each other out in a dull stalemate. Lineker scored for us but Kevin Sheedy equalised and I think Bobby realised there had to be changes with Holland coming up next in Cagliari, formidable opponents at the best of times and firm favourites to beat us.

Bobby took the bold initiative of dropping Stevens and, in reverting to a 3-5-2 system, brought in Wright in defence and me at wing-back. This was a position completely foreign to me, not having even played there in club matches, but I was more than happy to try. Trevor Steven was the obvious choice to play in that position but I think Bobby wanted a more defensive player and one who could adapt during a match if an alteration was required. I have no doubt that in my selection and in making major changes, Bobby listened to the opinions of his senior players.

Other managers might have seen this as a weakness but Bobby had around him a group of players who had been playing internationals in some cases for six or seven years and they knew what it took to succeed at this level. Bryan Robson was close to Bobby but I think it was Chris Waddle who advised Bobby to tighten the midfield – and he did. It might surprise some people to know that Sir Alex did the same with Robson, Roy Keane and Steve Bruce often consulted by him, out of strength, not because he had no idea what to do.

Holland were undoubtedly the best team I had ever faced up to then. They were effortlessly brilliant in all positions but my nerves disappeared once we kicked off. I did what I was instructed to do and that was to keep it simple. "Do what you are good at," Robson told me. I even got forward far enough to set up a Lineker 'goal' but it was ruled out for offside. Lineker won't thank me for recalling this, but he had a stomach upset and he dragged his backside along the ground at one stage like a dog.

My direct opponent and I tended to halt each other but I by no means disgraced myself and we got away with a creditable, though goalless, draw. Our only problem concerned the inspirational Bryan Robson who strained an Achilles and who had only played against the Republic after a painkiller dulled the pain from a toe injury. He later flew home for treatment, a second successive World Cup for "Captain Marvel" ruined by injury. I will let you into a secret about that toe injury of his. It was widely reported that he injured his toe in a match but in fact he had dropped a cast iron bed leg on it during a lifting contest at the team hotel. Just as well that never became public knowledge at the time.

The two draws meant we had to beat Egypt to qualify for the second round. Egypt were seen as makeweights in the group but our manager made sure we never believed that. I remember how tense we were before the start and during the match because there was no free-flowing football or chance to show why we were supposed to be a superior footballing nation. It was settled by a Mark Wright header from a Gascoigne free kick on the hour but the Egyptians made life difficult for us and we had to work hard to see them off. They had a couple of brothers playing for them and, for all Bobby's words of caution, I was surprised how capable they were as a team. But we were through, and that was all that mattered.

Belgium in Bologna was our reward and my own reward for some solid contributions was a place in the second round starting line-up, still as a wing-back. Bologna was a beautiful ground with its own church and a long passage underneath to get from the pitch to the dressing room and I remember noticing how I no longer felt nervous. I sat in that dressing room listening to Soul to Soul on my headset, oblivious to the outside world. It was a sort of ritual I had developed during the competition and I was not about to drop it now with a possible final no longer a pipe dream.

As soon as we came out on to the pitch in front of a huge and vociferous crowd I got racist abuse from the Belgian fans and, I fear, from some of our own as well. I found it bemusing that the Belgians should stoop to this but luckily it made little difference to my performance. Enzo Scifo was an arrogant opponent but a brilliant one, twice almost scoring, but I felt he was upstaged that day by Chris Waddle. Chris was a top-class player at the height of his career. He was a calming influence in front of me and he made my

World Cup a whole lot easier by his encouragement, his positioning and his great skill. Odd that he never faced me directly during our careers and I also never took on John Barnes.

David Platt, with a truly magnificent goal on the swivel from a free kick by Gascoigne, won us the match in the final minute of extra time. Platt would never have scored a better or more important goal but Gazza played his part with a wonderful free kick, taking a long run-up and then slowing before drifting the ball in for Platt to convert. Seconds later the match was over and I had never known such an outburst of emotion. There was a night of immense celebration, starting in the dressing room where the normally parsimonious Robson allowed us a couple of beers and continuing back at the hotel where we sneaked many more into our rooms, the adrenalin flowing and there was laughter and banter into the early hours as we relived Platt's moment-of-a-lifetime and our own contributions to the downfall of a very good team.

Our revelry was tempered in some measure by the fear of the press. There was a fear they might knife us in our finest hour, as they had done to Bobby Robson and to Steve McMahon who had been accused, I believe, of getting involved in some corporate activity during the championships. Michael Hart, a respected reporter with the *London Evening Standard*, had always been good to me and after the Belgium match back at our hotel he started talking to me as we sat on the stairs. The next thing I knew was that Gazza had drenched us with a bucket of water. He screamed: "Headlines...Parker has water thrown at him." Hart did not take offence and nor did I because it was Gazza being Gazza. One-to-one he was a great lad but any more than two people became an audience for him.

There was a sense, at times, of mutual suspicion between the players and the press because we had stuttered rather than swaggered through the competition to that point and it is true we had not played at all fluently. I knew a fair number of the reporters already and I got on well with Pat Sheehan of *The Sun*, Ben Bacon, Rob Shepherd, Barry Flatman, Hart and Stammers and the photographer Bob Thomas. I saw no reason not to speak to them because there had been no individual criticism of me – I would have been informed from home if there had – and I have always believed it is the duty of players to speak to the press, and through them the public, win, lose or draw. Players are happy to talk when they are winning but not when things are going badly and the press remember that. You are a small cog in a big machine and I realised after I had retired that you have to give sometimes.

Cameroon were our opponents in the quarter-final, the first African country to reach the last eight. Howard Wilkinson was our scout and his verdict was: "You have got yourself a bye into the semi-finals." But it was never going to be that simple, especially as Cameroon had beaten the holders Argentina, sensationally, in the opening match of the tournament. No country reaches the quarter-finals by luck and we took his observation with justifiable scepticism.

We got to the stadium in Naples and 45 minutes before the kick-off Bobby Robson simply disappeared. Robson had been shattered and drained by the whole World Cup experience – and all that had gone before it – and we discovered later that he had found a doctor's room with a couch and curled up and gone to sleep. Don Howe, unable to find him, took charge, gave us our last-minute instructions and then prepared to send us out on to the pitch. It was clear Don was worried about us because we did not look like a side ready to do battle.

There was an air of false security developing, not helped when the star-struck Cameroonians wanted to swap shirts BEFORE the match had even taken place. They were clearly in awe of us as we lined up in the tunnel, staring at us not in menace but like fans. Just as the referee prepared to lead us out there was a loud shout emanating from one of the side-doors and from it came Bobby Robson. Bleary-eyed but refreshed, our manager gave his instructions along the lines of "England expects" and off we went.

Not that his words made much difference because we gave a distinctly lethargic performance and we were surprised how good they were. Cameroon were leading 2-1 with only eight minutes to go and I think we pulled through only because of their naivety and our extra mental toughness. They gave away two penalties needlessly and with more experience of the big occasion I feel they could have held on and beaten us. One of their players was clean through at 2-1 and only his desire, I recall, to finish with a flourish stopped him nailing us. At 3-1 there would have been no way back.

My header into the penalty area led to Lineker being fouled for the first of his two penalties and once we got it back to 2-2 I think we were always going on to win. Had we lost it would have been the biggest upset in the tournament and I remember thinking how fans at home must have been feeling as we floundered our way through the match. The whole episode was embarrassing from start to extra time finish and the talk afterwards was of relief and escape. How would we have got home if we had lost? As for Belgian-style celebrations, they were long forgotten.

Teams don't reach a World Cup semi-final without a measure of good fortune and we certainly had plenty of luck against Belgium and Cameroon. We could have been dead and buried in either of those matches but we survived, I believe, through our will to win and our experience. Later in our ill-fated semi-final against West Germany, we did not have the rub of the green but then, in my view, we had used it all up in our previous two fixtures. There can be no complaints in that department.

Against Cameroon we carried injuries to Des Walker and Wright but we got through because when it mattered we had the right people playing for us at the right time. None were more effective than Gary Lineker, a striker in his prime and an independent thinker, strongly motivated to succeed and a world-class finisher. I am not surprised Gary has done so well in the media because he was always interested in its workings and cultivated those within it who were influential. You would always want Gary on your side in a big match but you had to play to his strengths, namely to get the ball in front of him so that he could run at the opposition. When he did that, Gary always stood a good chance of getting you a goal. Any player who finishes with 48 from 80 internationals has to be taken seriously.

Gary did not like training and he did not like playing in five-a-sides. All he ever asked as a player was for others to get him the ball facing the goal and it was a single-mindedness which served him well in a long and productive career. There was an aura about Gary as a person. He could be quiet and he could be quick-witted. Like some of those in the Queens Park Rangers dressing room, he could be a bit cutting in his remarks and you had to be careful what you said or how you said it. But he always gave the impression that he knew what he wanted out of life and in his case it was a post-football career in the media.

There were other strong characters in that England team of 1990 and some excellent footballers. Lineker was ruthlessly efficient in front of goal but Waddle was a wonderful player, Platt got his golden goal, Shilton was nearing the end at 40 and after clocking up more than 100 caps, Robson was a fantastic midfield player when fit, Beardsley was an elusive little raider, Walker had great pace for a defender and in Pearce there was a remarkable competitor at left-back.

But of them all, the one I most admired was big Terry Butcher in the centre of our defence. Without doubt Butcher was the most patriotic player I have ever played alongside. His battle cry was "come on lads, we're caged tigers". Bellowed at full blast, he had this capacity to lift us all with this shout and in time he became our talisman and a great leader who drew instant respect. We all remember that vision of him with his blood-stained bandage around his head. It was the perfect summary of him as a player and as a person because it was so typical of his determination to play at all costs. Off the field he was a gentle giant; a pleasant fellow who was liked by us all, but if ever a man personified on the pitch what Bobby Robson stood for, it was big Terry. Opponents were intimidated by him and I think Walker was fortunate to play in the centre of defence with him. All Walker had to do was pick up the pieces. In the more modern era, Tony Adams was the nearest to him. England were lucky to have them and they remain two of the most unselfish players I played with.

But for every winner there has to be a loser and ours in Italia 90 was Neil Webb. Webb played 26 times for England and was a great success in the First Division with Brian Clough's Nottingham Forest and to a much lesser extent at Manchester United. There in Italy it became clear that Webb was not going to get a game unless there were many injuries. For a squad of 22 to succeed in a tournament such as a World Cup it is essential that those players not in the starting line-up support those who are. They must also stay fit and be as prepared as the first-choice players.

I started the finals outside looking in and finished it as an established player but Webb appeared to take it personally when he was excluded, locking himself away and sulking. There were inevitably others who were also left out but none showed their disappointment as publicly as Webb. Those of us in the team understood how he felt and sympathised as much as we could but his bitterness was obvious and when he made no attempt to hide his feelings it did nothing for collective morale.

Steve Hodge was another outsider, in his case because of injury, making him something of a passenger. Because our room-mates had been sent packing by Bobby Robson at Burnham Beeches, we were teamed up for the finals and he was a strange companion. Through Hodge I got to know his Nottingham Forest team-mates, Pearce and Walker, and his greatest desire seemed to be to get away from Forest. We were given a telephone allocation in those pre-mobile days and it was always good to ring home and get a dose of domestic reality. Hodge had no family and used his allocation to ring his mum or his agent to see if there was any interest in him. He was a likeable lad but was a glutton for punishment and Pearce took every opportunity to give him some verbal stick while I nicked his phone allocation since he was hardly using it. He also had an annoying habit of cutting out the crosswords from newspapers so that he could do them and no one else could. But, in fairness to him, he supported us and that is all we asked.

So all that stood between us and a place in England's first World Cup final for 24 years was West Germany. As I explained, we failed, but the whole tournament was a fabulous experience and one that left me walking on air for months. I was treated like a hero when I got home everywhere I went, everywhere that is except at Queens Park Rangers.

Chapter 6

Venables and the hotel phone call

BOBBY GOULD had been a robust centre forward in his playing days with Coventry and Arsenal and went on to manage a startling number of clubs with the same determination and enthusiasm he had shown as a player.

Nowhere did he achieve more success than at Wimbledon in the glory days of the Crazy Gang. It was Gould who led the team out at Wembley in May 1988 when the Dons created one of the great upsets in FA Cup history, beating Liverpool 1-0, a match in which Dave Beasant saved a penalty from John Aldridge.

But my first meeting with Gould was less than happy. Don Howe, for some reason, had taken him on as assistant manager in late 1990 while I was recovering from a serious knee injury. Queens Park Rangers in those days were one of the sweetest passing sides in the First Division and, prior to Gould's arrival, we had some great passers while I was at the club – people like Ossie Ardiles, Ray Wilkins, Peter Reid and Nigel Spackman – with other high-class players including Colin Clarke, Gary Bannister, David Seaman, until he was sold to Arsenal for £1.3m, the emerging Les Ferdinand and many other excellent footballers.

But the introduction of the bombastic Gould changed our whole philosophy in three brief months. Gould wanted us to play like Wimbledon, whose long ball game and fierce competitiveness had divided football opinion into those who sought to emulate it and those who hated what they were doing to the beautiful game. Gould seemed to think he had invented the Crazy Gang concept but it had been Dave Bassett who initiated the astonishing Wimbledon progress from non-league football to FA Cup winners in little more than a decade.

Credit to Gould for what he did at Wimbledon but it was partly thanks to him that I endured my worst season at any club. I had been looking forward to getting involved again after a hernia operation and then my knee injury but Gould's first words to me were: "You're a big-time Charlie now and I don't like big-time Charlies." Why he said that, I do not know, but I am bound to say in my defence that I have never been that sort of person. I replied: "I played for QPR before the World Cup and I am playing for them afterwards."

If his purpose was to alienate me at a stroke, he had succeeded. Not that it would have done him any favours in the long run. Word soon gets around in the small world of football and it is unwise to make enemies. To this day, I don't know why Howe employed him but from the first training session he tried to impose on us a regime and a style which had worked perfectly well for Wimbledon but was unlikely to do the same with us. We were different players, not unreceptive to change, but it was against our nature to want to kick the ball down the other end of the pitch and chase after it.

One of the things he insisted we did to help build muscle and team morale, presumably, was to play rugby. I like rugby and admire those who play it, but that is not what we were paid to do and the grimace on the face of the venerable Ray Wilkins as he emerged from the bottom of a scrum will live with me forever. Perhaps Gould felt threatened by my presence, that of an England international, because the Wimbledon ethos of togetherness and collective aggression had been built on having no star names, no one who might consider they were better than their team-mates. As a result, I think he wanted to push me out of a club where I had always been very happy by confronting and belittling me.

I started only 13 league games that final season, 1990/91, because of injuries but if there was a compensation for a double hernia and then a damaged cruciate knee ligament it was that I did not have to work with Bobby Gould. Make no mistake; all I wanted to do was play for Queens Park Rangers. There were no thoughts of me using the club as a stepping stone. Things may have turned a little sour at Fulham near the end of my time there because of the financial mess but I was always loyal to the cause, and so it was with Rangers – until Gould came along.

The double hernia, one either side of my groin, had been developing throughout the World Cup finals of 1990. It is a condition known now as Gilmore's Groin after the famous surgeon who identified it and sought a cure. I could feel it worsening throughout the finals and the only way of playing through the pain was with the aid of the masking drug cortisone. Gilmore himself used to administer the cortisone and the pain was so terrible I remember digging my fingers into his hand as he did it. Having just got in the England side I did not want to drop out again so swiftly and then miss the life-changing final stages. But I was scared, and I knew that when I got home I would soon need an operation and a spell of recuperation.

I was admitted to the Princess Grace Hospital for repairs at the same time as Paula Radcliffe's husband and there were three of us having similar surgery. It was a delicate and difficult time. Urinating was an involuntary and painful action and we feared laughing or coughing all the five days of our incarceration. With hospital bands on our wrists we waddled off one day, like saddle-sore cowboys, to the nearest pub and for daring to make light of our predicament, we were threatened with an enema. We did not do it again.

I came back too soon from that injury and I knew that was the case when we played Manchester United and Mark Robins turned past me in a way no one had done for years. I was feeling my way back gradually when I suffered another major injury and this time I was out for five months. Don Howe, for reasons best known to himself, insisted I played in a low-key match at Southampton in the Zenith Data Systems Cup in November 1990, an extra competition for First Division clubs which had a Wembley final but failed to provoke much interest among players or spectators before its demise.

Tony Roberts was our goalkeeper and, in colliding with him, I tore anterior cruciate ligaments in a knee. Luckily, if there was any luck involved, the tear was about 80 per cent. Any more, and I would have needed an operation and that would have meant up to a year out of action. Specialists wanted to send me to America for possible surgery but in the end it was decided no repairing operation was needed. I did take the opportunity to have a cartilage removed, a relatively minor procedure, and the worst part of it all was the enforced, long-term rest to allow the knee to mend.

By now I was living in Billericay, the other side of London to Loftus Road and, with my knee in a brace, it was hard to drive round for treatment and, with Gould waiting for me at QPR, I found a physiotherapist on the east side of London to begin the task of getting fit again. My saviour was Mike Varney, the former Spurs physiotherapist and now consultant to QPR, and I worked with his son, a one-time deep-sea diver, on a cybex machine, a sort of chair, at the clinic in Enfield where my legs became stronger than ever before.

I have no doubt that this injury, which wiped away a crucial stage of my career, delayed my departure from

Queens Park Rangers. I returned to find Jan Stejskal, the Czech international at £625,000, had replaced Seaman – and he was nowhere near as good – and the feeling of the whole club had changed, not for the better. I must emphasise how committed I was to Rangers but the club had somehow got completely the wrong impression of me. Bobby Gould had persuaded them I wanted to leave and said so, and I fear the club's fans had also decided that I would be the next to quit.

In between my hernia and my knee injury, I did at least score my only league goal for the Hoops in a 6-1 thrashing of Luton on 15th September, exchanging passes with Andy Sinton before firing a low shot into the corner of the net. Jim Ryan, later Fergie's assistant at Old Trafford, had apparently told his players not to worry about me if ever I got into an attacking position.

Luckily, Gould lasted only three months before becoming West Bromwich Albion manager, but the damage had been done to my position, and my departure was further hastened by Howe's resignation in May 1991. It would be only a matter of time before I followed. Gerry Francis, an England captain as a Queens Park Rangers player, was Howe's replacement and I saw out the season with him. I think we both knew our relationship as stand-in skipper (I had replaced Wilkins temporarily) and manager would not last long. Sadly my injuries meant I missed our first win at Anfield, by 3-1, at the end of March and returned on April Fools Day as a substitute against Derby without a panicking ram in sight. We finished 12th and I have never been more glad to see the back of a season.

Meanwhile Graham Taylor had replaced Robson as England manager and that also resulted in a complete change of style and attitude, mirroring to some extent what had happened at Queens Park Rangers. It all began quietly enough, the transition smooth and seamless, with a friendly against Hungary on 12th September at Wembley with a goal from our new captain, Gary Lineker. Taylor had resisted the possible desire to tamper at this stage and the team was made up by those who had come so close to winning the World Cup a couple of months before. Shilton and Butcher had retired and the team was Woods, Dixon, Pearce (Dorigo 46), Parker, Walker, Wright, Platt, Gascoigne, Bull (Waddle 74), Lineker and Barnes.

I was now some way back to full fitness after my hernia operation and I retained my place for the Euro 92 qualifier, a 2-0 win over Poland. Lineker and Barnes got the goals. But by the time I was next fit enough after my knee injury to play in an international, against USSR at Wembley on 21st May 1991, much had changed in my absence. I played against my future Old Trafford team-mate Andrei Kanchelskis in a 3-1 win but the team inherited from Bobby Robson was already being disbanded and replaced. Against Russia, Dennis Wise, David Batty, Geoff Thomas, Alan Smith and Ian Wright got their chances and not all of them were as good at international level as they were for their clubs.

What Taylor was doing was a deliberate attempt to fashion an England side in his own image. Taylor had been a tremendous club manager at Lincoln, Watford, mainly, and Aston Villa but this was uncharted territory for him. Unlike Bobby Robson who had a distinguished international playing career, Taylor's was distinctly lower division, finished by injury at Grimsby when he was 24. Admittedly the World Cup squad was not youthful but he took on an awful lot of quality when Bobby Robson quit for PSV.

Taylor had a club manager mentality and did not trust us in the way Robson had done. Robson used to smile and wave from a hotel foyer as we set off for the night for a few drinks in our England tracksuits. "Remember, you're representing your country," he used to say. Once he was out of sight, we used to rip off the tracksuits to reveal jeans and casual clothes. It was a bit underhand but he would have known that we would never have done anything to embarrass him, the England supporters or our country.

One of the first things Taylor did was to appoint the recently-retired Peter Shilton as goalkeeping coach but there was more to his role than that. I am not alone in being convinced that Shilton's real task was to inform Taylor of all the old harmless pranks and ruses we perpetrated under Robson. Shilton was no less guilty than the rest of us in that respect but once Taylor had been informed of our ducking and diving routines, it all changed. In short, he did not trust us. This was a shame because if there is no trust, there is no basis for a working relationship. We were not talking here about 18-year-old apprentices, but about seasoned professionals who by definition were the best in the country at what they did.

Almost immediately we were no longer allowed to use our private cars when staying with England so that he could watch our every move and it was his failure to treat us as adults, which I think undermined his management style.

I had been spoilt working under Robson and a year on from Italy, in preparation for the USSR friendly, it was clear the next generation were not as good as the last. It is always a temptation for a manager to change what he has inherited but I think Taylor should have made that change more gradual. I admit I may have been at fault in that I was not happy to accept the turnover of players and the alteration to our methods. I think I was slow to adapt to Taylor's way of business. I had played with Waddle in front of me and now there was not the same calibre of player, and in my view we did not play the sort of football expected in internationals.

Peter Bonetti replaced Shilton as goalkeeping coach, his job done, but Phil Neal was the only other member of Taylor's staff with any kind of pedigree at the top level. Taylor's assistant was Lawrie McMenemy, another man who had done well as a club manager, but had no experience of what it requires to be successful with England.

To some extent I have sympathy for Taylor because the job was something of a poisoned chalice in that there was still a sense of excitement and almost euphoria after Italia 90 and what could the new manager do to beat that? Win the next World Cup? So, as he began the task of replacing Robson's heroes with what he hoped would be a few of his own, he learned brutally of the old adage: England expects but does not wait. From day one, Taylor was under pressure from the public and from the press where the infamous turnip cartoon held him up to ridicule. In truth, the players he brought in, who did well for their clubs, were not of the same class as Robson's squad, the squad he was now breaking up.

At the end of a gruelling domestic season I was selected for the tour of Australia and New Zealand where we beat the Aussies 1-0, courtesy of an own goal, and then the Kiwis by the same score with a Lineker penalty. England have notoriously sent weakened teams Down Under but it gave unexpected international caps to players like David Hirst, Earl Barrett, Brian Deane, John Salako and Mark Walters, none of whom were later able to bridge the gap and forge full-time England careers. In fairness to Taylor, there was not the class around so some of the criticism of him was not altogether deserved. From my point of view, after the domestic problems at Queens Park Rangers, I was just glad to be involved with England, Taylor and all.

Gerry Francis also had the job of breaking up a side at Queens Park Rangers, a side that had been as successful as a club of its small size dared expect, and had been told that for every player sold, he could take home ten per cent. It was a team in decline, selling its assets and I knew I was on his list of players to be removed.

You would never call Gerry dapper. Scruffy might be a better word. He also perpetrated what we came to know as "Terror Tuesdays", a day of remorseless, worthless running from the edge of one penalty area to another to simulate match conditions. It was ridiculous that a man of his background, 12 times capped, should make us slog, monotonously, all morning for no obvious purpose other than to build stamina. Les Ferdinand and I inevitably trailed behind the others, cursing every pointless step. Our game was based on pace over a short distance and not on the box-to-box running which was the job of the midfield players. I understand he instituted the same schedule at Tottenham when he went on to manage them but I never saw anything like it in the best part of two decades in football.

As the season, 1990/91, drew to a close I was aware that clubs were showing an interest in me and checking my fitness. With cruciate ligament injuries, you can never be sure of ever returning to your best and they have been known to finish careers. My last game for Queens Park Rangers, as it turned out, was against Everton on 11th May 1991 when Tony Cottee was my direct opponent. Cottee had scored four times in his previous three appearances but I marked him well and he was eventually substituted. Any watching scouts would have seen that my troubles were behind me.

I went home for the summer fully expecting to be sold at any stage but in the long hot days of June and July nothing happened.

Had I not been convicted of drink-driving on New Year's Day 1991 I would probably have joined Arsenal. I was driving my BMW on the A12 near Chelmsford the morning after a heavy night. I was speeding when I overtook a brown Granada which just happened to be an unmarked police car. It was eight hours after my last drink and when I blew into the bag I was one point over the limit. Back at the police station a blood sample also showed me to be the tiniest margin the wrong side of freedom. Well-intentioned police officers 'advised' me to ask to go to the toilet and do some press-ups to work up a sweat and rid myself of the alcohol but I thought they were taking the p**s in a different way and rejected the opportunity, somewhat arrogantly. A second test showed I was fit to drive home but it was too late.

In those days to be successfully breathalysed the morning after a drinking session was unheard of and I was both embarrassed and hurt, so much so that I was too scared to go home and tell my wife. Instead I headed for the Crown at Billericay in a belated attempt to gather my wits and decide what to do next. I was banned for a year and fined £200 and, of course, the court case appeared in the papers on 6th January, my mother's birthday. Mum gave me the biggest rollicking of my life, every bit as fearsome as Sir Alex's hair-dryer. The worst part is that I was sat in a car (not driving), stationary on the M25, soon after my conviction, when a person in the car alongside held up another newspaper which gave a full report of my ban and the court proceedings. Underneath it was an article analysing the way footballers drank to excess. My humiliation was complete.

The point of the story is that when Arsenal came in for me later that summer I was still banned and getting to the training ground would have been very difficult from my home in Essex. Maybe I am looking for excuses because I don't think my heart would have been in signing for Arsenal. They were the first club to agree a fee with Queens Park Rangers, so it would have been tempting to go to Highbury, but the fact that I was not able to drive was a reason not to join them. Had I been driving, I might well have given in.

Truth be told, Tottenham were my team and I would have found it difficult playing for their old enemy. It just did not grab me. But, I concede, not many people turn down Arsenal. George Graham, the Arsenal manager, was already putting together a formidable defence and accumulated such fine players as Lee Dixon, Tony Adams, Steve Bould and Nigel Winterburn while David O'Leary was still around. I am not sure where I would have fitted in, but it is odd to think that I might have been a member of the famous

Arsenal back four which was to become an integral part of the team for the next decade.

I was in Sweden on a pre-season tour with QPR when Arsenal's interest prompted Francis to send me home to meet George Graham. I was by now fully fit but Francis kept me on the bench in the knowledge that it would only be a matter of time before I left. In one of the Swedish games I came on as a substitute and scored a goal. But that same night, a night out for the lads, I was on the plane to London. My possible move to Arsenal was all the more unusual because our chairman, Richard Thompson, was an Arsenal fan and so was our chief executive Clive Berlin. They were willing me to join the Gunners, having agreed a fee of £1.8m. George did what he could to persuade me but he offered me only what I was already earning with Rangers and there was no sponsored car, not that I was eligible to drive it.

In any case, Lee Dixon was the established right-back and although more direct in style than me, was now in Graham Taylor's England team. I was a centre-back in the international side and I think Dixon was more his sort of man. So there I was in a kind of limbo. The reason I returned from Sweden was to sign for Arsenal and now I had rejected them. Thompson and Berlin were disappointed, but the message from them was the same, that I had to go somewhere. The newspapers were enjoying themselves with columns of conjecture about my likely destination and they seemed to know more than I did, throwing in the names of all kinds of clubs and linking me with moves that were never likely to happen.

Sheffield Wednesday and Everton did get in touch. Wednesday were managed by Trevor Francis, once of QPR, while Howard Kendall went on record to say that he wanted me. As a result of Kendall's comments I started to get some very unpleasant hate mail from so-called Everton fans. In total, there were about half a dozen letters, obscene, ridiculous and malicious but the sentiment was the same: don't join us. One of them said that John Barnes was already on Merseyside at Liverpool and they did not want a black man playing for them. I wonder why it is that Everton appear to me to have had a smaller percentage of black players than most other Premiership clubs, but I can't be certain of that. Anyway, I got the message and crossed Everton off my list, not even speaking to Kendall about a transfer to Goodison Park.

This is not because of any overt racism but because my boyhood heroes Tottenham got in first. Terry Venables was their manager and the prospect of joining them was tremendously exciting. I remembered the years spent on the White Hart Lane terraces, dreaming like all the other youngsters, of one day pulling on the famous white shirt with the cockerel motif. How many of those youngsters ever fulfilled that dream? I had just become a partner in a wine bar in Brentwood, which is deep in Spurs territory, and my driving ban would not have got in the way. I even started making mental plans for my new Spurs team-mates to come along to the wine bar to give it a boost.

I was genuinely delighted at the prospect of joining Spurs and I went along to the Royal Lancaster Hotel in Central London at Venables' invitation to complete the formalities. My agent, Neil Ramsey, and I were convinced it was a done deal. Venables was in his element, joking and grinning and being the perfect host. Spurs had also agreed a £1.8m transfer and had no reason to believe they would fail to sign me. I was a Spurs fan, I lived locally and I had business interests in the area. What could be more convenient? In return they were getting an England international in his prime at 27 and desperate to play for them. The money Spurs offered was much better than I was getting at QPR – and, as it turned out, better than I got at Manchester United – and it was all going smoothly until my agent was told by a barman that there was a call for him. Even that did not interrupt the Venables flow until Ramsey returned. The call had been from Maurice Watkins, solicitor and director at Manchester United. Would I like to speak to them?

The mood of the meeting changed immediately. Venables suddenly became less convivial and sensing that I did indeed want to speak to United, uttered a phrase I shall never forget: "If you go up to see United, you won't come back." By that he meant that once I had been to Old Trafford, met Sir Alex and seen their facilities I was sure to join them.

Venables shook our hands, said his offer was still open and wished us well. Ramsey and I got in our car and headed north, leaving Venables to finish his drink alone, a beaten man. In fairness to "El Tel", he never bore a grudge and after I had agreed to sign for United, the hardest part for me was ringing him with the news. "Ok then," he said – and the phone went dead.

Even my mum and dad, non-football fans to the core, had heard of Manchester United, Bobby Charlton and George Best. Indeed when I was a 13-year-old associate schoolboy at Fulham, Best (then a Fulham player) used to drop me home on his way to see his wife Angie and her family in Southend. Now, unless there was a major hitch, I was about to emulate Charlton and Best in becoming a Manchester United player.

Chapter 7

Oven-ready for England

V ENABLES WAS right. From the moment I arrived at Old Trafford I knew I was going to join Manchester United. It was a hot summer Saturday and the car park was so busy I thought there must have been a game on. But, as I was to discover, this was not like any other club in England. There was no game and the cars belonged to fans who had just come to worship the football club they adored. There was the museum for them to marvel at the trophies and the array of caps, medals and shirts and there were the guided tours where they could explore every nook and cranny of the famous stadium.

Sir Alex met me and would have made a perfect tour guide. He knew everything about the club and how it worked. As we wandered around the outside of the pitch, a group of fans were sitting, staring out at the empty pitch as if they were watching the grass grow. A woman spotted me with Sir Alex and shouted: "Are you going to join us?" My wits had deserted me and I replied: "Yes." In retrospect, I should have kept my mouth shut or mumbled a "dunno" but Sir Alex had me hooked. "Oh, you've decided then," he said with a smile and a wink and probably made a mental note to offer me less money.

Tottenham did come up with a better deal but finance was no longer a consideration when I agreed to join United. The only consolation I can offer Spurs fans is that I would not have signed for anyone else but United, and if they had not been involved, the main part of my career would have been spent at White Hart Lane.

Sir Alex was completely straight with me, told me where he wanted me to play and of his vision for the team of the future. By coincidence, Peter Schmeichel had signed on the same day and, in time, my wages improved in line with our success. The £1.8m received by Queens Park Rangers was a club record for them and I presume Gerry Francis collected his ten per cent. With the driving ban and with my wife and daughter back in Essex, I lived at the Midland Hotel (where George Best was an occasional visitor) in Manchester and discovered how everyone wanted to talk to me about football and United. It was hard to have a quiet drink because everyone claimed a bit of your time, in the nicest possible way.

I am not alone among Londoners in discovering with some sense of surprise how much football means outside the capital and particularly in the north. In London, even as an England player, it was possible to go out to pubs and clubs and either not be recognised or simply left alone. But in Manchester I quickly came to understand that there was an almost religious aspect to the game. There was the family and there was football. I know Les Ferdinand felt the same when he was sold by QPR to Newcastle.

I flew out immediately after signing to join my new team-mates in Austria where I was part of a team beaten 5-1 by Austria Memphis the following day. Four days later I played in Matt Busby's testimonial against the Republic of Ireland. That match ended 1-1 and I was just about ready for the 1991/92 league season, my first in the red shirt of Manchester United. By subsequent United standards, it was good without being great. We won the Rumbelows

Cup (the League Cup) and were runners-up to Leeds in the First Division in its final season before the Premiership was introduced and replaced it. Sir Alex's classic team was beginning to take shape and we were starting also to look like an outfit to rival the one produced in the halcyon years of Busby, Charlton and Best.

It is hard to believe Notts County were in the same division that year, bearing in mind their rapid demise, but they were our opponents on 17th August 1991, and we beat them 2-0 in the first of my 26 appearances. One of the low points of that season, and in fact my whole career, was losing 4-1 at home to QPR on New Year's Day, one year to the day after I had been picked up for drink-driving. How the R's fans must have enjoyed my humiliation and who could blame them?

It all started to go wrong for me and Manchester United the day before. We stayed in a hotel overnight on New Year's Eve even though the match, one of the first to be televised live by Sky, did not kick off until 5pm. We trained on New Year's morning while most sensible people were sleeping off their hangovers. It was obviously a big game for me but there was no time to relax and I could see that, as a team, we were oddly lethargic and tired. I could see it in the players' faces. Rangers ran us ragged and my old room-mate Andy Sinton caught me as cold as I have ever been caught. Sinton was nicknamed "the rat" for his scuttling running style but the real Rangers hero was Dennis Bailey who scored three goals. It was another 14 years before David Bentley of Blackburn scored the next hat-trick against United and that was not at Old Trafford.

At the end of the game, the triumphant Bailey got hold of the match ball and came into our dressing room to get it signed by the United players in the time-honoured fashion. Steve Bruce, who had been his direct opponent, got hold of the ball, said "don't be silly" and threw it out through the door.

I started the season at United at centre-back because Gary Pallister had been injured in pre-season and I soon discovered how good a player Bruce was. With all the players given caps, deserved or undeserved, by Graham Taylor, it is bizarre that Bruce never got even one, going into retirement as the best uncapped defender of his generation. England were well off for central defenders, it is true, with Tony Adams, Mark Wright and, before them, Terry Butcher. But I still find it strange that he never got at least one chance over his ten years at the top domestic level. I suppose Bruce was no great stylist and his detractors would have said he was not at his best on the ball but I believe this to be nonsense. I think his skill level was very underestimated and his other qualities far outweighed his faults.

I must admit, after our incident at Gillingham when he put me into the stand, and after playing against him when he was at Norwich, I thought that he was a nasty centre-half. Steve was not big by today's standards or especially quick but what I came to like about him was his bravery and his willingness to lay his body on the line for the team. John Terry is the only centre-half anything like him now, perhaps the last of a dying breed of defenders who are not scared to get hurt and who dominate the play around them. Too many of today's defenders are happy to let the ball hit them but are not prepared to climb over bodies to get in first.

Some of the present, very expensive, defenders are not in Bruce's class when it comes to the fundamental requirement of a centre-half in getting in front of the man he is marking. Bruce's oft-broken nose is testimony of his desire to win the ball, an old-fashioned centre-half who gave everything for United in every match he played. It was not his nose which caused him problems when I was alongside him, it was his thighs. He was always complaining about how his thighs hurt and sometimes he used to limp out to play, but we were always relieved when he was in the team. When he was not, we didn't win and that said all you needed to know about him.

Above all, he personified Sir Alex's approach on the pitch and provided, as an example, everything that the manager demanded of the rest of the United team. Bruce did his best to ensure he got it. One of the most pleasing aspects of our accumulation of trophies was that any kind of success was new to Steve Bruce. At Gillingham and at Norwich and in the early years at United, he had little to show except a League Cup winner's medal in 1985 for his 100 per cent honest commitment and endeavour, so that once we started collecting cups and medals he was entitled to enjoy every minute. In the days when we were regular visitors to big matches at Wembley, Steve used to say on the coach: "We're nearly there now boys. I can smell the hot dogs." He said it every time without fail.

As an England player, Wembley was not unknown to me, and it was always a thrill to be there, but it was a strange experience heading for the twin towers with my club, as I did in April 1992 for the League Cup final, sponsored that year by Rumbelows. It was a big occasion for United fans because there had not been the kind of consistent success expected of a club of our size and stature within the game.

We beat Middlesbrough over two legs in the semi-final to set up a final against Brian Clough's Nottingham Forest and, although it was no classic, we won 1-0 and the team's 'novices', me, Peter Schmeichel and Kanchelskis, collected our first domestic medals. The nearest I had previously got to Wembley for a final was a semi in the Simod Cup in 1989 and a quarter-final in the FA Cup a year later, so this more than vindicated my decision to sign for United. Going home on the train to Manchester was a fantastic feeling and there was a growing realisation among us that here was a team emerging who might be making regular trips to the home of English football. Steve Bruce would be smelling a lot more hot dogs.

That season I also had a little taste of European football, the first two rounds of the European Cup Winners' Cup before elimination, but I became so wrapped up in the United ethos that playing for England, so vital to me at Rangers, became almost an afterthought.

About a month after signing for United I played at Wembley for England against the newly-constituted Germany, a match we lost 1-0 after conceding an early goal. For me, it something of a setback because I tweaked a hamstring and carried on somewhat naively instead of getting myself substituted at the first available opportunity. I had never sustained a hamstring injury before and my foolhardiness proved costly because it restricted the number of matches I played for United and led, indirectly, to me being left out of all Taylor's international squads for the next two years.

At Wembley that day I should have put my club first but my ego and pride of performance drove me on to the final whistle. Only when I was recuperating was I told that the hamstring problem was almost certainly a compensation injury for my cruciate ligament trouble but, by then, Taylor had written me off. I don't know if Taylor had some kind of grudge against me or if he could detect my cynicism at his methods and style, but I drifted out of contention, partly because of the injuries, and missed the European Championships in Sweden the following summer.

In a funny sort of way, I'm not sure if I was that bothered. Playing for United was demanding, more demanding than anything I had ever known. Every game was a big one because Manchester United were always the team to beat and, with a big squad available to Sir Alex, we all wanted to play at every available opportunity. If you were injured, as I was too often in my five years at Old Trafford, you could feel very left out and isolated. At smaller clubs, like Rangers, playing for England was something extra, something special, but when you played for Manchester United it was as if every match was an international. My priority, therefore, over what should have been my peak international years was to get fit for Manchester United.

In any case, I think as a choice for the right-back position, Taylor preferred Lee Dixon. He was more Taylor's sort of player, getting the ball forward at greater distances than I had become used to at Old Trafford, and more often. At United, I was encouraged to pass over shorter distances, perhaps ten yards, and leave the clever stuff to more able players. Taylor liked a more direct style and Dixon fitted that requirement better than I did. He also appeared to like his goalkeepers to kick the ball down the pitch instead of, as Schmeichel liked to do at United, throw it to the nearest defender to begin the process of building attacks. So from my point of view, playing for England came close to being a chore.

Many of the great players I knew from the Robson era had either got old or had been replaced and there were far fewer characters. Taylor liked to create a good team spirit by filling long evenings with mock casinos and karaoke sessions. Oven-ready chickens were the prize on one occasion but I was not a gambler, no money ever changed hands, and I found most of what happened tedious and pointless. You had to enjoy your football to give your best and I did not enjoy being with England any more and, while that might sound unfair or ungracious, playing for Manchester United was a full-time occupation and we were treated by the management there with far greater respect.

I know for a fact, without naming them, of players who feigned injury so that they did not have to join Taylor's England party, and others arriving as late as they could while also pleading injuries. Robson let us go to the pub, as I have pointed out, but it was clear Taylor would never do the same. Other stalwarts noticed the change, how the old camaraderie had gone, but of course the newcomers had nothing to compare it to and were happy enough simply to be playing for England.

Little things changed. For instance, Dr John Crane, the squadron leader as we called him, was England's doctor. He loved England and he loved Arsenal where he worked and, without exception, the England players thought the world of him. He was always cheery, always pleasant and, besides being good at his job, also boosted morale. One of the ways he did that was by making sure all the players were properly fed. He was always worried that we did not eat enough and made sure we finished every meal, leaving nothing on our plates. On his rounds at Burnham Beeches, our training headquarters, he used to come to us with bars of chocolate to help energy levels and because he liked dishing out treats like an indulgent father. His laughter and his jokes were much appreciated by the players in the Robson days, as much as the bars of chocolate. When Taylor took over, Dr Crane lost his food job and, with it, the keenly-anticipated chocolate round.

Once I had recovered from my hamstring injury and time passed, it became obvious that I was simply not being selected for England any more. I was sorry to have missed Euro 92 and I admit to feelings of envy when the squad was announced, whatever else I might have felt about Taylor's regime. If it was going to be anything like Italia 90, I was going to be absent from a great occasion and from the incredible environment inevitably created by a party of top-class players preparing intensely for a major tournament. Fergie always had numerous players away on international duty and he was always relieved when they either returned home uninjured or were not selected, as was happening to me. If I had still been with Rangers, I would have felt very sore and hurt at not being in the squad but I can say honestly, after the initial pangs of envy had died, that I was not greatly concerned.

At Manchester United, I was aware already that two defeats in succession was bordering on a crisis and, for someone like me not used to such high standards, it was quite a draining experience in that first season at Old Trafford. All my energies were concentrated on getting into and staying in the team at United and conforming to the demands of a very big club. England was not my priority.

Gascoigne, Barnes and Wright were also missing from the England squad which had a poor tournament in Sweden. They drew without scoring against Denmark and France and there was no sadder sight, in my view, than Gary Lineker being substituted for Alan Smith after an hour of the defeat by Sweden, one short of equalling Bobby Charlton's record of goals.

Only about half the team which had featured in Italy with such distinction remained two years later, even allowing for injuries. I think Taylor might have been worried about my injury problems and, I must admit, I only played about nine times from February so there was in his mind a doubt about me. Sadly, England limped home not even having reached the knockout stages at the same time as I was still coming to terms with United's astonishing collapse in the league, a league we should have won.

How Leeds won the title that year I will never know. We drew with them twice in the league, 1-1 at Old Trafford in August and 1-1 at Elland Road at the end of the year, and beat them twice in the cup competitions, 1-0 at Leeds in the FA Cup and 3-1 away in the Rumbelows Cup so that our mastery over them was complete. But we still let them overtake us at the death and snatch the championship from our grasp.

Even now it is hard to recall the events of the last few weeks without a sense of shame and guilt. With four matches to go we were top and cruising but then it all went horribly wrong. We lost to Nottingham Forest, West Ham and Liverpool, while Leeds, seemingly destined for the runners-up spot, sensed their chance of overhauling us.

My last appearance of the season was in the drawn match at Luton four games before the end of the season and I still thought I would have a league winner's medal to go with my Rumbelows Cup prize. We lost 2-1 at home to Forest and 1-0 at West Ham, so we had to win at Anfield to revive our hopes before it was too late. Leeds had already beaten their Yorkshire rivals Sheffield United 3-2 and their players watched us, kicking off later, being taunted by Liverpool fans on the Kop, holding up banners to remind us just how many times they had won the league since our last triumph 25 years before. How they laughed as we went down to a goal in each half and our humiliation deepened when we learned how Eric Cantona, among Leeds players, had watched our latest failure on television on Lee Chapman's sofa.

It made no difference that we beat Tottenham on the last day of the season. It was too little and far too late. Leeds were champions over 42 matches and we were left with a terrible feeling of disappointment. I know the incredible way we fell away at the end of the season had a huge effect on our manager. Ferguson had a point when he blamed our pitch for our failure to win more matches at home because it cut up badly at times and we struggled for goals. In private moments I shuddered when I thought back to that shocking home defeat by Queens Park Rangers on New Year's Day. Luckily the margin between ourselves and Leeds was four points, otherwise I might never have forgiven myself.

Among us all there was anger because we had handed Leeds a title they had gained as much by our limitations as by their own achievements. The following season they fell away to 17th, escaping relegation by two points and that said it all. Was it lack of collective bottle? Was it lack of resolve? Was it the pressure of playing for Manchester United? I don't think it was any of those things. We were a bit naive, yes, but there were no players of weak character who might have capitulated when the going got tough.

Where I think we went wrong was our inability to change tactics or respond to a problem on the pitch. We were not

My mate Ian Hart and I before a game for my local cubs' side aged eight. Would you believe I was a prolific goal scorer in those days?

The Sanders Drapers School team in 1978. I am seated on the floor on the right hand side giving my best cheeky grin. The plaster on my left knee is a big give-away that I was injury-prone even at a young age.

I made my Fulham debut aged 17.

My performances against Liverpool in our epic Milk Cup third round tussles of 1983 alerted clubs nationwide to my ability to snuff out the likes of Ian Rush. We took the Anfield giants to two replays.

Here I am in one of my early matches for England under-21s playing against Romania in 1985. Pulling on the three lions blazer never failed to get me brimming with pride.

He who rises highest. Here I am out-jumping from left to right, my former Fulham team-mates 'Mr Sky Bet' Dale Tempest, Simon Webster and Paul Raynor playing against Huddersfield in 1984.

Mark Wright and I celebrate our 1-0 David Platt-inspired win against Belgium in the 1990 World Cup. Mark was an aggressive but elegant centre-half and I enjoyed playing alongside him.

This is how I earned the accolade of 'tackles like a ferret' from Bobby Robson, first clattering German skipper Lothar Matthaus in the 1990 World Cup semi-final…

…and then the man who whacked that ill fated free kick against my legs, Andy Brehme. This kind of tackle was outlawed by FIFA a few years later, I am sure I got the ball here.

Is it going in?

World Cup fame brought many spin-offs, including switching on the Regent Street lights with Gazza left (stealing the limelight as always with his shiny shell suit) and Chelsea's Tony Dorigo.

The one that got away. Alex Ferguson consoles a desolate United side after losing the 1994 League Cup Final to Aston Villa at Wembley. We would have become the first side to achieve a domestic treble had we have won.

Football can be a brutal game. Here I am being elbowed in the face by Australia's Tony Vidmar. Perhaps he thought I was an aborigine!

Ferguson, Busby and Kidd show off United's first League title for 26 years. The success was dedicated to Sir Matt. It was a privilege to have met him.

The two full-backs, myself and Denis Irwin, known as the quiet man because of his reserved approach to life.

Celebrating in the bath after being presented with our first Premiership title in May 1993. Water and beer don't mix.

United's marketing director Danny McGregor made the mistake of coming into the dressing room to congratulate us. Captain Ahab is on the side of the bath waiting to capture him.

Pride of place in my collection; me and the Premiership trophy. Spot the infamous navy blue and white striped jacket in the background.

Gary Pallister as you have never seen him before! Pally had nothing to hide except the £10 he would have handed me, but for his bet-saving final day goal.

Martin Edwards, club director Amer Midani and Fergie on an open-top bus tour in the wind and rain to celebrate our 1994 Premiership trophy.

A typical Manchester afternoon. Me and the late, great Les Sealey singing in the rain on the top of the bus.

My final international appearance came under Terry Venables' stewardship in a 1-0 win over Denmark in April 1994. It was Terry's first game in charge and I wish I had played more under him.

Sent off against QPR on the first day of the 1994/95 season, the beginning of the end of my United career. Here I am glancing over a youthful-looking Dermot Gallagher's shoulder for Les Ferdinand doing his 'dying fly' impersonation.

A bad night in Barcelona: United players trudge back after conceding the last goal in a 4-0 drubbing at the magnificent Camp Nou, when because of the foreigner restriction ruling many of our best players were left in the stands.

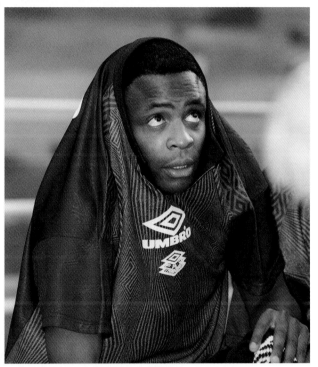

Me doing my ET impression during our pre-season trip to South Africa – I have just been asked to phone home.

And my United team-mates helping me to celebrate as I did not know how to.

Shaking Ferguson's hand before the manager's testimonial match at Old Trafford. He is asking me where all my hair has gone.

In action during a difficult time at Derby. I was still grieving for United.

Me being booked playing for Sheffield United in possibly the worst kit I have ever worn. I look like a bruised banana.

flexible enough and therefore lost matches we might have drawn and drawn matches we should have won. We did not, also, looking back, know how to handle the big matches. Too many of them eluded us when it mattered. All the while those questions about us remained; the title was as far away as it had ever been. Our manager reckoned we did ourselves a disservice by knocking Leeds out of the cup competitions, leaving them free to concentrate on winning the league.

One of the saddest aspects of the late collapse was the poor turnout in terms of attendance in the testimonial for Norman Whiteside, who promised as a teenager to become one of the great United players before a knee injury ruined and then curtailed his career before he had reached his prime. The match against Everton would have been a sell-out had we won the league a few days earlier but only 7,434 turned out for Norman's big match.

When we reported for pre-season training for 1992/93, Sir Alex Ferguson began our preparations by giving us a collective flea in the ear and there was no one who disputed his right to do so. His message was loud and clear: no losers, no sulkers and make sure you don't fail this time. We did not. Overnight we became mentally stronger and filled with a collective determination to right the wrongs of the previous season and it says much for the Ferguson imprint on our collective consciousnesses that the United ethos of success by desire and professional preparation remains to this day.

Overnight, we learned how to win matches, big and small, 1-0, if that was all that was on offer but our failure in 1991/92 was a very expensive learning process.

Chapter 8

League of
our own

MANCHESTER UNITED only signed Eric Cantona because Leeds were on the phone to Sir Alex trying to buy back Denis Irwin. When Leeds were told Irwin was not available, Sir Alex asked about Eric and was surprised to find out he could be bought for about £1m. In my view, and it's a view shared by all my team-mates of the time, the signing of Eric in November was the catalyst for winning our first league title in 26 years.

We should, of course, have been entering that 1992/93 season as champions but we fell away so unforgivably badly that we allowed Leeds to snatch it from us, and there is no doubt that the controversial Frenchman was a key player in their triumph. So to be able to buy him relatively cheaply was a huge coup for us, an absolute steal, and gave Manchester United a whole new dimension.

Eric was different. That was the best way to describe him. We all knew of his troubled background, how he had committed international suicide by falling out with the French football authorities and then come to England to escape and further his career. Trevor Francis turned him down at Sheffield Wednesday and must have wondered if he had done the right thing when Cantona's breathtaking skill, strength and stamina became so instrumental in the success at Elland Road.

Why did he leave Leeds? I think he was too big a character for Howard Wilkinson. I had come across Wilkinson when he was scouting for England in Italia 90 and I don't think Eric was his sort of man. Eric was altogether too much of a maverick for Leeds. He needed a larger stage for his talents and Manchester United were the perfect club for him, the place where he could strut his stuff and be recognised for what he was, a terrific all-round footballer. Eric was his own man and Sir Alex realised that and did not, at the same time, see him as a threat to the tight team spirit which had evolved at Old Trafford.

I found Eric to be one of the lads. He would join in the dressing room banter and laughed when we all laughed. His wife was an English teacher and Eric spoke the language perfectly except when he chose not to understand. Sir Alex had no difficulty in getting the best out of him because he could tell that Eric was not like most other players and therefore should be allowed to do things his way. Not everyone could have got away with that. A big dressing room requires a certain conformity but Eric was no rebel and he was not the type to rail against authority for the sake of it, whatever the French might have thought.

Eric had a unique dress sense, neither too flash nor too understated, and Sir Alex wisely let him wear what took his mood, even to civic receptions when the rest of us might have expected to sport club ties and blazers – and did so proudly. The boss let him get away with it because he knew he would respond where it mattered, on the pitch. There Eric gave everything of himself all over the pitch and for every minute of every match. I used to marvel at how he would demand – and get – the ball even when there were four opponents around him because he had the ability and self-confidence to see them off.

Football was a means of expressing himself, as much as poetry was to him in quiet moments away from Old Trafford. The art of good management is surely to allow the individual to flourish in a team environment without disrupting the team and that is what the boss was doing with us because Cantona was by no means the only strong character or even the one, above all others, who made us tick. There was Schmeichel, Bruce, Pallister, Irwin, Ince, Giggs, Kanchelskis, Hughes and McClair, the backbone of the team, and all of them excellent players and great individuals in their own right.

There was no middle ground with Paul Ince, either. Like Cantona, he was vilified and adored depending on where he was playing and, again like Cantona, he did not care what people thought of him. I had a natural affinity with Paul because we both came from East London from immigrant stock and owed football a big debt for helping us develop away from that sort of background. Paul had also been brave enough to start his career at West Ham and had emerged from it a stronger man.

Opponents did not like playing against him and away crowds took every opportunity to have a go at him but that was because he was so competitive and carried with him a fierce desire to win. Hate him or like him, well I liked him. Sir Alex also liked his abrasiveness and his determination but Paul was more than once the victim of the legendary hair-dryer treatment, usually for not obeying pre-match instructions. We all got it. It was best to take your punishment and get on with it. It was best never to answer back, after all he was our employer, because he was always going to win the argument and the boss only ever wanted what was best for the team. If you did not do your job you could expect a blast and you probably deserved it.

My attitude, if ever I was singled out, was to be extra determined to prove the manager wrong but others, less cowardly, might occasionally summon the courage to answer back. Brian McClair was very cunning. He used to disrupt the manager's tirade in mid-flow with a disarming: "You're right, boss," a comment which tended to defuse the rollicking and caused the boss to calm down. Not that McClair was taking the mickey because he was always extremely committed to United and, on the pitch, never went missing or shirked his duties.

Choccy, as we called him, as in chocolate eclair, was the cleverest footballer I ever knew. A university man before coming into football, McClair was as sharp as a razor and could take on anyone in an argument. I shared a room with him and he was a terrific bloke but even he drew the line at direct confrontation with the manager, as opposed to Ince who did not.

There was a fearsome clash between the boss and Ince at Norwich in the dressing room at half-time. Ince was getting the hair-dryer treatment for what the manager thought was a poor first half performance from our midfield man. But as the rest of us winced in our seats, Ince bit back. They stood toe-to-toe in a most amazing slanging match with Ince ending it by saying he would never play for Manchester United again. It needed the pacifying qualities of Brian Kidd to get him back on the pitch for the second half, cajoling him quietly and telling him how much the team needed him.

Had it been anyone less influential I am sure Fergie would not have let him go back out but that was typical Paul Ince, never afraid to stand up for himself. In the second half Ince was a revelation and was comfortably our best player, a driving, dominant midfield performance and, at the end of it, the manager was the first to congratulate him.

If ever I was on the receiving end, I would bide my time and then approach the manager and say: "Boss, can I have a word?" I would go into his office and he would show examples of what had displeased him on the video. There were never any rows and he would listen to my point of view and, if he was wrong, he would be gracious enough to admit it. I think people outside the club see him as a dictator but those, like me, who know him better can testify that, away from the heat of the battle, Sir Alex Ferguson was prepared to debate rationally. After all, we were internationals in the main and he respected a different point of view if he thought it was valid. At the end of it all, the boss never bore a grudge. Sir Alex had around him some big personalities – Ince, Robson, Keane (later) – and we would never have achieved all that we did if he had suppressed honest argument.

Fergie, while aloof when he had to be as manager, could always enjoy himself among us and liked nothing better than to play cards in a school that also included Irwin, Bruce, Robson and McClair at the back of the bus on the way home. I used to sit parallel to them with "Sparky" Hughes and Clayton Blackmore and watch and listen to them swearing and bemoaning their luck. Sufficient to say, Sir Alex was a bad loser and let us know in no uncertain terms if he did. But, essential to his management, was a basic core of wanting us to succeed for Manchester United. It was a simple enough philosophy, and if it meant the occasional public blast for a player, then so be it. The long list of trophies won shows that his methods were the right ones.

Indeed my one professional regret is that I did not join Manchester United and Sir Alex Ferguson sooner. I was 27 when I arrived at Old Trafford and I had been a professional for the best part of a decade. Once you were there, you never wanted to leave because, in footballing terms, you could never do better than play for United. Sometimes people forget that I also played substantially for Fulham and Queens Park Rangers. They know me only for my five years at Manchester United and, of course to some extent, England, but principally United. My whole profile as a person was raised as a result and even today, some ten years or more since I left Manchester United I am recognised in the street, treated well and, I hope, respected.

Not only was the first team squad as powerful as it had been for many years, the club's youth policy was about to bear a rich harvest of fruit. This was the class of David Beckham, Nicky Butt, Paul Scholes, Gary Neville, all of them to become in time United heroes and superstars. Add to them players like Keith Gillespie, Chris Casper, David Johnson, John O'Kane, Ashley Westwood and a fiery blond-haired lad called Robbie Savage and you had a crop of young players coming through simultaneously, the likes of which had not been seen at Old Trafford since the all-conquering and ill-fated Busby Babes of the 1950s.

Those who did not go on to become household names with United succeeded elsewhere at a high standard and even now it is seen as a freak of sorts that all of those teenagers should come together at the same time under the same roof. Our scouting network must have been tremendous. I think all the senior players were aware of them immediately and how special some of them were going to be. In return I think I can say they all respected and venerated the first team players.

I had a lot of time for Butt. I empathised with him because he came, like me, from a working-class area (in his case of Manchester) and had come through a hard upbringing. It gave him a hunger to succeed which I can see still remains as vividly as ever. One of his tasks as a trainee was to clean my boots, as I had done at Fulham for the professionals, and that year I was sponsored by the boot manufacturer Asics. At the end of that season I gave him those boots and it was like Christmas, so pleased he was.

Of them all I thought Paul Scholes was going to be the best. In those days he was a little ginger centre forward but he was clever and brainy and there was a nasty streak about him, which singled him out as a bit different. I kicked him once accidentally in a practice match and, before long, he kicked me back and, as he ran away from me, there was a knowing smirk on his face. He knew what he had done.

We could all see Beckham's range of skills but I thought Scholes had a better all-round game and would be the bigger name.

Scholes, of course, did go on to become a key player in the next generation of United's success story under Ferguson, and played 66 times for England, but the Beckham story brought a whole new dimension to the expression footballing superstar. In my view, having seen him at first hand, I think Beckham has made the best of his talents but that his ability was not as great as some people think. I would place Cantona, Robson and Keane above Beckham as a midfield player. I would place Gascoigne ahead of him also. Gazza, for all his faults, was a great player who was ahead of his time in some respects. I think it was George Best who said Beckham had no left foot, no change of pace, couldn't tackle and couldn't head. To that I would add that he cannot run with the ball either.

Speaking as a defender, there was nothing more difficult to counter than a midfield player running at us from deep, making us decide whether or not to challenge and thereby leaving forwards unmarked. In this day and age, accolades like "great" and "world class" are used too freely. Zidane and Figo are world-class players, Beckham is not. Beckham is, at best, a high standard Premiership player, as were Cantona and Bryan Robson in the old First Division, but in my opinion they were not eligible to join the elite and be labelled world class.

Gazza could take on players in midfield, beat them by skill and run at defences, as could the Laudrup brothers and Roy Keane who had all the attributes needed to call himself the complete midfield player. Roy could adapt to any game situation and later, when he lost that edge of pace, changed his style and methods to cope. Beckham is a big-game player, that I would not dispute, and credit to him for making the best of himself and going on to become a genuine superstar. It certainly helped that he married a pop star and learned how to manipulate a voracious press with their constant fashion and hair changes.

Again, I understood him better than most because he was also from East London and I think he soon became the club's resident wide-boy, the Cockney geezer with the ready smile. When all that group of youngsters were promoted to their first professional contracts, part of the deal was a sponsored car each. I think I am right in saying they got Ford Fiestas from a local garage. Most of them would have been grateful not to have had to catch the bus any more but Beckham decided his looked too drab and ordinary so he went back to the garage and got himself some alloy wheels and other, what he considered, essential accessories.

The car park could be seen from the restaurant at the Cliff, the club's training ground, and as the boss looked out and around, his ever-alert eyes alighted on this souped-up Fiesta and he demanded to know to whom it belonged. I think he must have guessed. Within seconds Beckham was being told in Fergie's unique way that he should go immediately to the garage and get it replaced by a more conventional model. A decade later Beckham was travelling by private jet.

On another occasion, Beckham decided to wear white football boots at training and our manager saw this as a gross act of non-conformity, ordered him to take them off and then threw them over the fence into a garden next door.

Not that the boss was especially hard on him because he could see that here was an exciting young player and the last thing he wanted to do was crush a free spirit. I think Sir Alex saw all the youngsters in some way as his own surrogate kids and was protective of them. Giggs, at 17, looked like he could become a world-beater but he was a level-headed lad and had no desire to seek the showbiz-style limelight in the way Beckham did. Giggs had the talent to go somewhere like Real Madrid, if that was what he craved, and Lee Sharpe might have taken the Beckham route to international fame until he fell away. I don't think Sir Alex had quite the same hold over Beckham as he did over Giggs and Sharpe and later, when he became more prominent within the game, Beckham's PR took him on to a new level.

I had a lot of time for Giggs who came from a fractured background and had obviously gone through a hard time growing up. Giggs was mentally strong and mature for his age and you could spot immediately a great desire in him to be a top player. Nothing was going to stop him. He could also be a bit of a ducker and diver when it came to authority, but he prospered from having so many old hands around him and went on to become a great servant for United and Wales. There was always a part about him, though, that he kept private and even today everyone would love to know more about the real Ryan Giggs.

What I liked about being with a provincial city club like Manchester United was the togetherness of the squad, which was a fairly disparate crew assembled from all over Britain and beyond. We all socialised and the families went out together and enjoyed each other's company. This was just not possible in London where players came from different parts of town and the suburbs and it was a major task, with taxis involved, to organise a collective night out. For instance, I lived in Essex and I played for Queens Park Rangers on the other side of London. With the capital's roads, I could sometimes be in my car for up to three hours to get to Loftus Road and more still to the West End. In Manchester, from my home at Bramhall in Cheshire, it was never more than 30 minutes to the training ground, Old Trafford or the city centre. It was so easy to get around and a refreshing change from the way of life regarded as normal in London.

We all got on well with each other and I am sure that raised morale which was a contributory factor to our success. When the players went out for an evening together, we all chipped in with £10 for a kitty. In those days you could have a good drink for a tenner but Eric always put in £20. Eric drank only champagne, and plenty of it, so we figured he should pay the extra because we were all on lager and other less expensive drinks.

There was also the factor of accountability. In London, if you had a bad result or your team had lost, it was possible to hide. In Manchester, wherever you went, there was sure to be a United fan to let you know where you had gone right or wrong. This closeness gave us a sort of family feeling and it was that which Sir Alex was keen to encourage. It was always made clear to me that if you gave body and soul for the United cause, the club would look after you. If you have not let United down, the boss always welcomes you back.

But woe betide you if you ever crossed him as our former full-back Colin Gibson did by selling a damaging story about United to the tabloid papers. Sir Alex threw him out of the Cliff and made it clear he was no longer welcome. Anything reflecting badly on United was an unforgivable sin. When I left United in 1996 I was offered a lot of money by one paper to say something nasty about the club and those that ran it, but it was an easy decision to reject the offer. My reward, as such, is that I still work for the club on their television station MUTV but, in any case, I would not ever have said anything detrimental about Manchester United because that is not the way I felt about them. Even so, it is a golden rule. If you say anything bad about the club, you can expect to be ostracised.

One of my big pals was our Danish goalkeeper, Peter Schmeichel. We arrived on the same day, as I said, and we took in the United experience at the same time, trying to come to terms with one of the world's big clubs. Peter was sometimes obnoxious, sometimes arrogant but he had a heart of gold and we all loved him. As a goalkeeper, there were few peers. He would command his area and would shout and scream at us in the back four, but at least you knew where you were with him.

Peter and I used to hug each other after our wins and our families also became very close. I remember him being very kind to my daughter, Georgie, who used to play as kids with his youngest daughter, as an example of the way United players and families stuck together.

Peter was very poor at holding his drink and, on team nights out, we used to have to send him home early, always the worse for wear. Jimmy McGregor, our physio, used to rile Peter by calling him "the German". To him, a proud Dane, this was just about the worst possible insult, but we used to say that with his blond hair he must be German and I'm pleased to say it made him furious. Peter also sported a large red nose and we told him he must have been suffering from gout, but he took it all in good spirit because he was as dominant off the pitch as he was on it.

At 6ft 3ins and weighing 15 stones, Peter used to surprise us how fast he could run and indeed he was as quick as anyone in a sprint. During pre-season at the Cliff we used to have a competition to see which of Schmeichel, Cantona and Giggs could win over 100 metres. Eric, incidentally, was prone to coming back from the summer break more than a little overweight. But Peter was often the winner and, if he was, we all knew about it.

One of the first things I noticed about Peter was how good he could be with his feet. He had a lot of natural skill so that if we played the ball back to him he was entirely capable of looking after himself. Peter did not make many mistakes, but, if he did make one, it was often a big one. As an ex-handball player, Peter had strong wrists and he liked nothing better at the end of training than to get his deputies to shoot at him, as hard as they liked, from close range. There was a net behind him to give an air of reality.

Gary Walsh did as he was told and dutifully powered one shot after another at Peter's body. But Les Sealey had a sense of mischief and we used to plead with him to give us all a laugh by hitting the ball wide of Peter's body and into the net. This drove our first-choice goalkeeper mad, as we hoped it would, because the purpose of his game in his own mind was never to concede a 'goal'. Les used to pretend to apologise when all hell broke loose but he knew what he was doing.

Peter was a top-class, dedicated professional and could have played in any country had United not discovered him first and brought him over from Brondby. But when I look back now I realise he was just one of an incredible array of personalities we possessed at that time. They were all a bit unusual and yet, when they came together, they created a wonderful football team, well capable of winning the championship as we did for the first time in a quarter of a century.

My personal highlight of that season was my only goal for Manchester United. It came against Tottenham at Old Trafford on 9th January and you will forgive my indulgence while I relive it, swapping passes with McClair before beating Erik Thorstvedt with a cross-shot. Spurs were beaten 4-1 that day and it's slightly ironic that one of my four league goals (in around 400 league matches) should be against my boyhood heroes. When I got a return pass from McClair I saw two unmarked team-mates in the area, but I was determined to go it alone and have a shot. After running from deep in my own half I had no intention of setting up a chance for someone else.

I played in 31 of our league fixtures and, after losing our first two games to Sheffield United and Everton, we were consistent over the rest of the season, always in and around the top three, but what won it for us was an incredible late sequence of seven successive victories. Where our nerve had failed the previous season, we showed this time we had learned a valuable lesson in coping with pressure by beating Norwich, Sheffield Wednesday, Coventry, Chelsea, Palace, Blackburn and Wimbledon.

Not that we needed to beat Wimbledon because we were already in possession of the championship by then. With two rounds to go, it was between us and Aston Villa and it was all getting pretty exciting. On Bank Holiday, 2nd May, Villa were playing Oldham at Villa Park and were expecting to keep the pressure on us by beating a team who eventually finished a lowly 19th. Luckily, Oldham needed to win to stay up, so there was plenty for them to play for. We were playing Blackburn the next day at home. Villa's match was being televised, so I went to Steve Bruce's house near my own in Bramhall to watch it.

Bruce was doing a "captain's log" for a television company anyway, so there were cameras already in place in his sitting room as Oldham took the lead and then held on to win 1-0, a victory as vital for them as it was for us. Suddenly, we were champions without having kicked a ball. It was almost an anti-climax because we would have preferred to have clinched the title in grand style, but who was complaining? As the repercussions of Oldham's win became apparent, others players started to drift round to Bruce's house and supporters gathered in some numbers outside to join in and witness the celebrations.

Other television crews, hastily despatched to our captain's house, began to arrive and what had once been a peaceful afternoon in suburbia, turned into an impromptu house and street party. There was a great deal of drink consumed by us all that afternoon and evening, players conveniently forgetting that we had a match of our own next day. The party went on long into the night and it was only the following morning, when I awoke with a throbbing headache, that I realised I had a job to do in the afternoon.

I was not alone among United players in getting a taxi to Old Trafford that lunchtime, severely hungover, anxious to avoid bright sunlight and not knowing whether to feel ill or deliriously happy. Ill was winning. Needless to say, we were appalling in the first half, absolutely terrible. I gave away a free kick from which Kevin Gallacher scored. I also brought down Gallacher in the area, but luckily the referee ignored it, and at the interval, in front of an expectant but muted and puzzled crowd of 40,447 we were lucky to be level at 1-1 with nothing to play for, and then only because of a fantastic free kick from Ryan Giggs.

If it's possible for 11 players to get the hair-dryer treatment simultaneously, then we got it. The manager was furious and we sat there, pulsating heads hung in shame, as he dished out an almighty ticking-off. I just wish he had said his piece a lot quieter. "Win it," was his message and we went out determined to improve our wretched first half performance.

Somehow we drew on our reserves of stamina, shrugged off the drink-induced lethargy and responded to the desperate pleas of our fans to win the title in a manner befitting champions. They had waited long enough. I am pleased to say we were much, much better after our tongue-lashing and went on to win 3-1. At 2-1, and with seconds remaining, we got a free kick on the edge of the Blackburn area and the lads decided Gary Pallister, the only regular outfield player not to have scored that season, should take it. I was not very happy with this idea and even less delighted when the big man blasted his free kick through the defensive wall for our third.

At the start of the season, Gary and I had a £100 bet as to which of us would get the most goals. Being 6ft 4ins and sent up for corners, Gary must have been firm favourite, but after my goal against Spurs, I was close to being £100 richer. This left us with the Wimbledon match to decide a winner but neither of us managed to get on the score-sheet and the money was taken from my grasp.

After the final whistle Steve Bruce was presented with the league trophy and the famous old stadium erupted in joy. Each player was presented with a replica of this, the first Premiership trophy, and I could never get away from the feeling that it looked not unlike one of those you get from pubs for winning darts matches. But each one was worth £1,100 and I have since been offered £5,000 for mine, an offer I was able to reject without much thought. Eric Cantona's would have been worth far more, such was his fame, and probably still is.

One of the more pleasant and surprising aspects of that last home match came when Fergie decided we should not wear club blazers and allowed us to dress as we desired. This prompted a competition among the players to come up with the most bizarre outfit. I found a navy and white striped jacket and matching waistcoat and was duly crowned champion but it was so vile I never wore it again. I gave it to a charity shop.

Our final league match was at Selhurst Park against Wimbledon and there was a crowd of 30,115 – the majority United fans – to see us win 2-1 and finish with 84 points, ten ahead of Aston Villa, the runners-up, and 12 ahead of Norwich in third place. All that remained to complete a hugely enjoyable season was the traditional open-topped bus through the streets of Manchester. For two weeks it had not rained in the city, which in itself is a rarity, but on our big day, of course, it poured on our parade.

We were drenched, but the hardy souls of Manchester came out in their thousands along the streets to applaud, and none of us cared about being so wet. My beer kept being 'topped up' by the torrential downpour but it did not matter because the club had waited so long for this moment and we were all going to enjoy it, fans and players alike.

Chapter 9

United's Double delight

NELSON MANDELA helped kick off the biggest season of my career. For no obvious reason, the South African hero and black icon was something of a Manchester United supporter and insisted on being in our team photo and knew the names of all our players when we began 1993/94 in buoyant mood on a pre-season jaunt.

We played Arsenal in Johannesburg and lost 1-0 and then drew 1-1 with South Africa's big team, Kaiser Chiefs, in front of an incredible 65,000 near-hysterical fans, also in Johannesburg. Arsenal were also our opponents in the Charity Shield on 7th August and, for the first time in the competition, the match went to penalties. Roy Keane, our £3.75m signing from Nottingham Forest, made his senior debut and converted one of our spot-kicks. We won the penalties 5-4 after the match had ended 1-1 with Schmeichel easily saving a weak effort from his opposite number, David Seaman.

As usual when it came to penalty-taking, I was a long way down the list, crossing my fingers the fate of the shield would be decided before it was my turn. I was, therefore, a medal better off already and the season had not begun in earnest. Before it had ended, nine months later, I had added to it with a league winner's medal and another for winning the FA Cup – and there was almost a fourth. Only our failure in the final of the League Cup prevented us completing a clean sweep of all the domestic trophies.

It was also my most productive year in terms of appearances for United and, at 29, I felt on top of the football world. Even Graham Taylor was obliged to recall me, on the weight of performances, to the England side, but in this game you can never take anything for granted. There was a problem in the shape of increasing pain in an ankle, but there was no way I could, or wanted, to rest it. Competition for places at United was predictably fierce, and because of the fear of losing my position, I was determined to get on to the pitch at all costs. As it was, only the dreaded cortisone got me out there, time after time.

The problem with cortisone is that it gives you a false sense of well-being. Properly administered, it gets you through a match but only afterwards, once the effects have worn off, does it become clear that the basic injury is not getting a chance to heal. There are lots of players of my generation and older who have limped into middle age, the worse for over-using cortisone. I don't limp, but the damage is there. The ligaments in my ankle became badly over-stretched and the weakened foot is now inclined to collapse on me on an uneven surface. It needs to be strapped if I am involved in anything physical like playing veterans' football. I told you earlier how my shoulder, so often dislocated but now repaired, also causes grief in cold weather so that not a day passes when I am not reminded that my success as a footballer came at a price.

Our success at Old Trafford was based on having a settled side with Schmeichel, Pallister, Bruce, Irwin, Kanchelskis, Ince, Keane, Hughes, Giggs, Sharpe, Cantona and myself appearing together in most of the matches and McClair and Robson still very much part of the squad. The record books show that the 14 of us each played in ten or more Premiership matches and it was that continuity which enabled our manager to field pretty much the same side every week with variations.

Given the hectic schedule, it was a miracle so many of us stayed fit, and out of red and yellow card trouble, for so many matches. Towards the end of the season, when we were chasing the Double, it seemed like we were playing every day. In addition to the 42 games in the Premiership, we were also involved in nine ties in the Coca-Cola (League) Cup, seven in the FA Cup and four in Europe. A grand total of 62 and that fails to take into account the Charity Shield and four other big games in pre-season including Benfica and Celtic.

Roy Keane was an inspired signing. Of all the British players available that summer, Roy was the one we needed above any others. Bryan Robson was 36, and inevitably coming towards the end, and it was never going to be easy to find someone of a similar dominant personality. In Roy Keane, we found him. We had, of course, been aware of Roy's combative qualities at Forest but did not realise just how good he was until he came with us to South Africa.

From day one Roy was loud, opinionated and lovable. For the next 12 years he was the heart, soul and driving force of Manchester United, the manager on the pitch, respected and feared by opponents, vilified by their supporters and adored by ours. The press tended to demonise him, and it's true he was no stranger to disciplinary problems, but the Roy Keane we knew was very different. You would have thought that arriving in a dressing room filled with experienced, established stars any newcomer would have quietly bided his time before making his mark. But not Roy.

Roy got straight in among us with the same brash, in-your-face attitude which won him, outside the club, a host of admirers and a legion of enemies. We all took to him immediately. Roy liked boasting but, whatever he promised, he was determined to deliver. Here was a young man in a hurry. He wanted to reach the top and nothing was going to stop him. Sir Alex had his problems with him but never important problems and then only because, with his extrovert nature, there were bound to be confrontations with authority, big and small.

Just think of our midfield going into that season when it included personalities as strong as Keane, Robson, Cantona and Ince. How our rivals would have liked even one of those. No cause was ever lost, no task beyond us, no match ever conceded. Sometimes Roy gave me the hump with the things he said but he was always challenging us as much as he challenged the opposition.

Roy loved a drink in the early days, as we all did, and we looked forward to our sessions after a match or in midweek if there was no match or training to worry about. They would be called bonding sessions now in today's psycho-babble but we just enjoyed each other's company and put away an awful lot of alcohol. As I say, at my London clubs this just would not have happened. But here in Manchester, we had some wonderful times as a team group, feeding off each other and laughing the night away. I miss that now and I imagine the others must also.

But Roy, being the individualist he was, always insisted on walking home after a boozy night out. As the rest of us piled into taxis or got lifts, Roy used to set off into the darkness on his own, spurning all offers. We never knew why, perhaps to walk himself sober, but it was a habit which was somehow typical of Roy. On one occasion we had been at a nightclub, Yesterday's, and, at the end of the evening, Roy set off as usual on what must have been as much as seven miles to his home at Alderley Edge. The next day, Roy showed up for training at the Cliff with his face covered in scratches. He was a bit coy about the reason. Then the police showed up and chatted to Sir Alex before leaving, problem apparently sorted.

Only then did Roy reveal how on the way home he'd had a fight with a passing German in some bushes. The German had complained to police but the matter did not develop and never became public. But that was Roy, abrasive, belligerent, competitive. We loved being around him because he was always interesting, always doing or saying something provocative, always arguing, but once we were playing, there was no one you would rather have had on your side. If you failed to do your job on the pitch, he told you so fiercely because he always did his. Over the years he mellowed, inevitably, and I was sorry to see the way he left Manchester United. It was a bit of an anti-climax after all he had contributed, but these things happen in football and you can't necessarily go out the way you would have liked.

Europe was our one true failure that season. We were competing in the Champions League, rebranded from the European Cup and open only to those clubs who had won their respective leagues. Manchester United had an honourable record in the competition having won it at Wembley in 1968 when George Best was in his prime. It was, of course, on the way back from a European Cup match in Belgrade that the plane crash occurred at Munich in 1958, which temporarily ripped the heart out of the club.

In 1993/94, ties in the first and second rounds were still decided on a knockout basis over two legs and then the group stage began. Kispest Honved of Hungary were our first opponents but we were not greatly extended, winning 3-2 in the first leg out there and 2-1 at home. The second round drew us against the Turkish club Galatasaray and even now I shudder at the recollection. I will never go to Turkey again after what happened when we travelled to Istanbul and even now it baffles me why other people seek it out on holiday.

We should have crushed them at Old Trafford after racing into a 2-0 lead, but some sloppiness in defence (I can say with a clear conscience for I was injured and not playing) let them back in and they led 3-2 until Cantona equalised with nine minutes left. Cantona's equaliser also preserved the club's unbeaten home record in Europe, a record which would stay intact until 1996. So although the scores were level going into the second leg, Galatasaray had the priceless advantage of three away goals.

"Welcome to the hell" said a banner draped inside the stadium, and hell it was. Not that there seemed to be any problems when we first arrived in Istanbul. We stayed at a superb hotel near a bridge which links east and west, Europe and Asia and the waiters could not do enough for us or be more deferential. But from the moment we made it clear to them we had no tickets to give them, the whole atmosphere changed dramatically. Their attitude changed completely and from doing everything for us, they decided to do absolutely nothing for us.

It was even worse when we got to the ground. The hostility and intimidation we encountered was genuinely frightening and I seriously wondered if we would escape with our lives. Police took away lighters, knives and other weapons as Galatasaray fans made their way to the stadium with mayhem on their minds. An hour and a half before the start, the stadium was filled to its 40,000 capacity and they were singing blood-curdling songs against us. Nothing in England had ever prepared us for the intensity of this kind of hatred, and it was hatred. You expect opposition crowds to tease and torment, but this had a nasty edge that had nothing to do with football rivalry.

We had an experienced, worldly-wise squad and there was not much we had not witnessed at some stage or another, and been able to shrug off. This was different, mesmerising even, and football suddenly seemed remarkably unimportant. I was glad not to be a spectator because our supporters had bottles, rocks, cans, everything thrown at them and, trapped under a wire mesh roof, were spat at and urinated on by the locals.

Nor was it any safer on the pitch. I was playing as a central defender and was booked for pulling down Tugay as the Turks used every means possible to waste time, the onus being on us to score at least once. Tugay eventually came to England to play with some distinction for Blackburn but that night I found him arrogant and mean-minded, using every trick possible, some of them legitimate, to disrupt the flow and disturb our attempts to find any kind of rhythm.

As the final whistle neared and with the score still 0-0, a frustrated and incensed Cantona pushed over a member of the Galatasaray bench who was trying to prevent him getting the ball to take a throw-in. It was typical of the whole miserable night and when the Swiss referee Kurt Rothlisberger called a halt to the game, we were almost pleased even though it meant we had been eliminated. But even then it was not over. Cantona gave the referee a blasting in French for not adding some extra minutes because of the blatant Turkish time-wasting. Unfortunately the referee, a French teacher, understood every word and decided that Cantona was accusing him of cheating.

As the Galatasaray players hugged and we headed for the dressing room without so much as a polite handshake, Cantona got a red card. Cantona was a Turkish target from first to last and, as he and Robson headed down the tunnel, they were attacked by the people they thought were there to protect them, namely the baton-wielding police. Cantona had his head pulled back and was punched and Robson needed stitches in a hand wound after being struck by a riot shield.

They were not alone. As I made my way through the belligerent throng, I was struck by a stick, I think a policeman's baton, across my back and only the safe hands of Schmeichel prevented me falling down eight or nine concrete steps. We had to count the players in the dressing room to make sure we had all survived and even then our ordeal was not over. On board the coach we felt no safer, either, as jubilant Galatasaray fans banged on the side, attempted to rock it and threw anything they could lay their hands on at us while the police made no effort to intervene. At the airport there was no security and we had to wait the best part of three hours before they allowed our plane to leave. I never found out why we had been detained but we all believed it was deliberate. I am never going back.

Two months later, in January 1994, the great Sir Matt Busby died and the whole of Manchester was plunged into mourning. Even City fans bowed their heads for a man who personified all that was good and great about Manchester United. Sir Matt was 84 but his death was still a shock and it was like part of the club and the city had died with him. Sir Matt was Manchester United in many ways and was comfortably the biggest influence until Sir Alex came along and revitalised the club in the 1990s.

Sir Matt was manager between 1945 and 1969, and briefly again in 1971/72, and during his reign Manchester United won the league five times and the FA Cup twice. The highlight of his managerial career was the European Cup success in 1968 after beating Benfica 4-1 with a team, which in addition to Best, also included the legendary Bobby Charlton and a young Brian Kidd in place of the injured Denis Law. A nation had prayed for him as he battled in a Munich hospital for his own life after the air crash ten years earlier.

After he stepped down and was elevated to president, he became a sort of club father figure and when we won the title in 1993, he emerged again as a focal point for supporters who had enjoyed little prolonged success since his retirement. I met Sir Matt and liked him and, while I was aware of his importance, I was unprepared for the outbreak of grief gripping the entire city. I have never known Manchester so quiet, as it was for a day or two after his death. All the players and backroom staff went to the funeral and it was a very moving occasion.

Our first match afterwards was at home to Everton and, such was the emotion, there was no way they were going to beat us. We pummelled them from the first whistle but got only the one goal through Ryan Giggs. I formed the strong impression that Everton did not want to win and knew they could not, and in all my years I had never witnessed an emotion-charged match like it outside the international arena.

How we did not end the season with a domestic Treble I cannot understand even from the distance of a decade or more later. It irritates to think how we let the Coca-Cola Cup slip away from us. We beat Stoke, Leicester, Everton, Portsmouth and Sheffield Wednesday and should have seen off Aston Villa at Wembley.

Ron Atkinson, the Villa manager, had been in charge at Manchester United until being replaced by Ferguson in 1986 so this was a big chance for him to prove a few people at Old Trafford wrong. What excuses can I offer? For a start, the grass was too long. It held up our free-flowing football, but there were other reasons. Schmeichel was banned and we missed him, although that would be unfair on Les Sealey, his deputy, who could not be blamed for our 3-1 defeat. Villa were soon two goals up and, when Mark Hughes pulled one back with seven minutes remaining, there was a genuine feeling we could go on and win. Then Dalian Atkinson's shot struck the arm of Kanchelskis on the goal line. Kanchelskis was sent off, crying, and Dean Saunders scored the penalty.

It may sound strange, but the Treble was not something we ever considered seriously and it was only after we had won the league and the FA Cup that we began to regret our Coca-Cola Cup near miss. It was all the more galling because I don't think Villa were the better side, beating us on the counter-attack.

Mark Hughes got us into the FA Cup final so it's him I have to thank for my winner's medal. We were fortunate even to be at Wembley for the final because it was seconds away from being Oldham, and not us, against Chelsea. The path to the semi-final was straightforward enough, beating Sheffield United, Norwich, Wimbledon and then Charlton in the quarter-finals. It's hard to think of Oldham as a power in the land, but with Joe Royle as manager, they were always tough opposition in their three years in the top flight and we knew not to expect an easy semi-final, which that year was also held at Wembley.

Oldham made sure we did not get one either, with a dogged, competitive performance and, after 90 minutes, it was all going nowhere at 0-0. Then Oldham scored in extra time, I was replaced by Nicky Butt after 108 minutes, and it needed a dying-seconds equaliser, a stunning trademark volley, by Hughes to prevent a genuine cup upset. In the replay at Maine Road, we had no trouble and won 4-1 to set up a potentially exciting final with Glenn Hoddle's Chelsea, who had beaten us twice in the league that year.

I will always remember that final for Chelsea's crazy choice of colour for their official suits. They wore a delicate shade of parma violet, which is a light sort of purple, and when all the players gathered in the centre of the pitch they looked to me like a Welsh choir. I went over to speak to Nigel Spackman, the Chelsea midfield player who had been a team-mate at Queens Park Rangers, and it started to rain, darkening and blotching his suit with every drop and making him look faintly ridiculous. It brings to mind Liverpool's cream suits of 1996, which Roy Evans told me made him feel silly.

By now we had already won the league, so we were pursuing the Double. Only three other clubs had won the league and the FA Cup in the same season in the 20th century and this was a fantastic opportunity for us to join them because Chelsea, for all Hoddle's cultured influence as player-manager, were not expected to beat us. Shedding their parma violet suits, Chelsea were level 0-0 at half-time and even came close to leading, Gavin Peacock's shot rebounding from Schmeichel's bar. But it was different after the break, Paul Ince took control of the middle of the field, the referee David Elleray gave us two penalties – Kanchelskis fell over like a tart for one of them – and we romped home 4-0. For the record, Cantona converted both penalties and the other goals came from McClair and Hughes.

That season I played in 56 matches for United, by far my most productive for them, and there were also a couple more for England, a little unexpectedly. I like to think Graham Taylor recalled me to face Holland in October 1993 for a World Cup qualifier because I had been in the form of my life but, having been excluded for so long, it was still a surprise. Taylor offered no explanation but I think he was backing my experience for such a vital match, an occasion for which Taylor became something of a national laughing stock for his "do I not like orange" tirade from the touchline as we slid out of the competition.

I found it hard to get involved having been out for so long and where I had Andrei Kanchelskis in front of me at Manchester United on the right side of midfield, in Rotterdam it was Carlton Palmer. Need I say more. A month later in San Marino, Lee Dixon was back in the England side and it looked like my international career was over. But in the intervening six months, Taylor was displaced by Terry Venables as England coach and the door swung open for me again. I have to admit I feared Terry might still bear a grudge after the way I had rejected him and Tottenham to sign at the 11th hour for Manchester United. He could have seen it as a personal snub because he liked transfer negotiations and to lose me in such a way, pen all but poised over the forms, must have hurt. But there he was, smiling as usual, full of genial chat, when I showed up at the training camp for the match with Denmark.

There was an aura about Terry and it was easy to under-stand why he excelled on television. The players liked him, too, because he was a clever tactician and he kept his talks simple, everyone aware of their task. Terry soon made me feel part of the squad, and I think I was efficient enough in helping us win 1-0, but it turned out to be my 19th and last international. Venables started to build his own squad and I drifted out of contention, never to appear again. I was just short of my 30th birthday and having my best ever season.

Should I have played more often for England? I think so. My caps were spread over five years from 1989 and, for one reason or another, often fitness, I missed a fair number of matches in that time. Bobby Robson's habit of making newcomers wait for their first chance did not help and Graham Taylor omitted me by choice. I believe my final tally should have been around 30 and if I have an international regret it is that I did not work more with Venables because it was obvious he was an exceptional and innovative coach. I know Ince and Pallister loved playing for his England side but I maintain that it would have been hard for me to play for England and United simultaneously. To that extent, I sacrificed my England career to give everything I had for the United cause.

To have played so many times for United, on the other hand, in their Double season was a highlight of my career and a privilege. My football years had two major focal points, Italia 90 and Manchester United's trophy-gathering resurgence so I had a lot to be grateful for. But my other regret from that season is that I was not more selfish over my ankle injury. While I was proud of being a United stalwart in an historic season, I knew I would require surgery on it sooner or later, it was just that the timing was crucial. All the while I was delaying the inevitable I was doing further damage to myself and, even in the summer of 1994, at the end of a momentous season, I chose not to go under the knife.

All I was doing was making it worse and, in the end, I have to say it ruined my career. I should have gone into hospital at the first available opportunity that summer and, had I done so, I think I would have played at the top for at least another three, meaningful, years, rather than be the passenger I ultimately became. But, stubbornly, all I wanted to do was to play for United as often as I was able and, for that, a heavy toll was taken.

The result was that I played all those games in 1993/94 with the fear that the injury would eventually catch up with me. But it was such a pleasure to be involved in a team as powerful as Manchester United at their peak. The more we won, the more I wanted to appear. We carried all before us in the league, topping the table by the end of August with 13 points from five games after Keane had scored twice on his home league debut against Sheffield United. We were still top at the end of September with 22 points from nine matches and never looked back.

In October we played Queens Park Rangers, always a big match for me, and on the night before the match I went round to the Rangers hotel for a chat with my old mate, Les Ferdinand. Les and I always got on well and we had a great evening together with all the jocular remarks about what we were going to do to each other next day. What I had not realised was that the manager had decided to put me into the centre of defence, which meant I was in direct confrontation with Les. There were no smiles or laughter now.

Within minutes, Les had shoulder-charged me so powerfully it knocked me off my feet and left me sore for days, and I was still shaken when he rose above me to head the ball into the path of Bradley Allen for the opening goal. I got a grip of him after that and we came back to win 2-1 but it was a nasty reminder to keep friends at a distance when they are also opponents. Les, incidentally, was a top-class forward, much feared in his heyday. I always felt he should have done a little better even though he played often enough for England and did several clubs proud, but to me, he was always a bit too laid-back and the desire to fulfil his talent was somehow missing. When he was a youngster at QPR, he was loaned out to the Turkish club Besiktas for a year and he loved it so much that he had to be told to come back.

The occasional jolt aside, our progress to the championship was serene because we hardly ever needed to make any changes. There were injuries but not long-term ones and the manager could chop and change as he desired without altering our overall performance. By the end of October we were 11 points clear of Norwich and Arsenal, and by the end of November that lead had improved to 14 points ahead of Leeds and Arsenal.

Nothing got in our way for long. On Boxing Day, we were one goal down to Blackburn and Fergie hauled me off after 74 minutes to bring on an attacker, McClair. Two minutes from time, Ince bundled in a Sharpe corner to earn a point. By the end of the year, Blackburn were our nearest rivals but they were a monster 14 points behind our total of 56.

In January we were the victims of an astonishing comeback by Liverpool. Bruce, Giggs and Irwin put us 3-0 ahead after 23 minutes but Liverpool clawed back to 3-2 before Neil "Razor" Ruddock levelled to complete a sickening turnaround. Memories of that match at Portsmouth in the wind were rekindled but by the end of January we were 16 points clear of Blackburn whose only advantage was that they had three games in hand.

Not even our considerable involvement in the cups impeded our progress, winning, to my delight, 3-2 at Loftus Road and Ince defying the barrackers at Upton Park to equalise with three minutes remaining. Not that I escaped completely, roundly booed for a booking, but we concluded February with Blackburn seven points behind us. Only in March did our 34-match unbeaten run finally come to an end when Gavin Peacock's goal gave Chelsea a 1-0 win.

Schmeichel was red-carded for handling outside the area in our victory over Charlton in the FA Cup quarter-final and I was the one who had to make way for his goalkeeping replacement, Les Sealey. Cantona was sent off controversially for two yellow cards in the draw at Arsenal, his second dismissal in four days, but nothing knocked us out of our stride for long and there was a tremendous resilience about the squad. Even if key players were missing, whoever came in did a more than competent job so that we were never seriously weakened.

After beating Liverpool 1-0 on 30th March, we went into the final full month of the season in a powerful position with only Blackburn dogging our footsteps and the glorious prospect of the Double remained within our sights. Blackburn seized their chance to remind us that nothing was yet decided by beating us 2-0 at Ewood Park where Alan Shearer rose above me for the first and then added another after I had been substituted. This introduced a sense of tension to the title race for the first time in a long season and we entered May with only three matches left still two points clear of Blackburn but we had a precious game in hand.

All we needed to do was keep our nerve, but our detractors were hoping that our involvement in the FA Cup might cause us to slip through fatigue. We beat Ipswich 2-1 after being a goal down, my quick throw setting up a winner for Giggs and, the next day, Blackburn handed us the title by losing to Coventry. We duly rounded off the league season with a win over Southampton and a goalless draw at home to Coventry where some young lads were given a chance. Gary Neville, among them, was the man who would one day replace me permanently. Indeed it was me who was dropped to the bench to allow him his first start.

Then came the Cup Final and the habitual open-topped bus ride through Manchester, parading the league trophy and the FA Cup, giving us another reminder of the joy football brings to the lives of millions as they lined the pavements on our route. At the end of it all, the bus dropped us off near the airport at a favourite bar of ours called Mulligan's and the party carried on through the night. After all, it's not often you win the Double.

Chapter 10

Hansen's Beckham blunder

IF THE Double-winning year of 1993/94 was the high point of my career, then the following season was the lowest – and I mean the lowest in every conceivable way. I was injured for most of it, I drank too much, my marriage broke up and I ended up feeling as though my entire world had collapsed around me.

There is no room in professional football for the long-term injured. There is real sympathy at the start but as the months drag by the club has moved on without you. Your position in the team has been snapped up by someone else and, no matter how hard you try, you cannot any longer share the successes and failures of people who were once your closest buddies and team-mates.

My horizons shrank, arriving early for physiotherapy, spending much of the day on my own and leaving late, long after the others had left for home or had headed off for a big match. And when we played at Old Trafford I was the forgotten man for much of 1994/95, sat disconsolately in the stands, watching and waiting for the chance to reclaim my rightful place among the Red Devils.

It was my fault, my stubborn refusal to sort out my right ankle, which had bothered me like an aching tooth for a year. Sir Alex Ferguson liked winners and I so desperately wanted to be a winner for him, but I knew my ankle had not improved with a summer's rest from the moment we reported for pre-season training. Remember, I was 30 and supposedly at the top of my profession, allying relative youth with a dozen years of experience, much of it at the top level. I reckoned I had at least another three good Manchester United years left in me and Sir Alex has been kind enough to say in his foreword to this book that, had I not been injured, I might have emulated Denis Irwin in playing for the club I loved until I was 36.

Sir Alex had instilled in us the same hatred of defeat, the pride of performance he expected from all players lucky enough to pull on the red shirt. Losing affected the lives of our supporters, he told us, and, whatever you did, you must not lose to Liverpool, Leeds or Manchester City. My relationship with him was always good although I once made the terrible mistake – and still can't believe I did this – of calling him "Taggart" during a training session. Taggart was a fictional Glasgow television detective, and there were similarities between him and the hero, Mark McManus, but it was a profoundly stupid thing to do and something I regret to this day. I think I was being egged on by a couple of the others and I knew as soon as I had said it, I had blundered. He responded by calling me a "f*****g little pygmy", which in the circumstances was fair enough. Why I did such a suicidal thing, I will never know. It's the sort of thing a 13-year-old child might say to a teacher and, while it raised behind-hand titters among my colleagues, it was never mentioned again. Ha, bloody, ha.

I knew something had to be done about my ankle in July 1994 when I went over on it during a testimonial in Dundalk for Gino Lawless, a setback which marred my entire season. I recovered enough to play in another testimonial, for our former player Clayton Blackmore at

Middlesbrough on 16th August, but the boss was aware I was struggling and named me as a substitute for the opening fixture against Queens Park Rangers. I wish I had stayed on the bench. Soon after coming on in the 70th minute against ten-man Rangers (Clive Wilson had been sent off for fouling Kanchelskis), I was also dismissed.

I think I am right in claiming a first here, the first player to be red-carded for the newly-created offence of the professional foul. My old friend and adversary, Les Ferdinand went down all too easily 25 yards from goal and I was deemed the last defender. I was off before many people realised I was on. I was never the most vocal of players, but I gave Les a blasting for that one and I think he deserved it. It was bad enough making history, but to be sent off against QPR hurt badly and the only consolation was that we won 1-0.

Suspension inevitably followed and my only league start in the whole season was in early October at Sheffield Wednesday where we lost 1-0. I was either being kept back by the manager for the European games or recovering from the operation which followed the match at Hillsborough. This should have been a great season for me in terms of what was in prospect. As league champions and FA Cup winners, we were defending our titles. There was also the League Cup, the one that got away the previous year, and, above all, there was Europe.

The rules of eligibility at the time were hardly designed to help those clubs, like ours, who were becoming increasingly cosmopolitan. The European Cup was now changing into the Champions League format and I was being kept back deliberately for the six matches in our league, home and away against Gothenburg, Barcelona and Galatasaray. The problem was that only five foreign players were allowed in each team for each match and that severely weakened us. Ryan Giggs of Wales and the Irishmen, Irwin and Keane, were classed as foreigners.

I know Sir Alex was desperate for me to play, he said so in his book, *A Year in the Life – The Manager's Diary*. He wrote: "I really want him to play in Barcelona. He is the player who could do a job on Romario for me. Very few players have the discipline, the mental toughness that Paul has. If I asked him to go and play against John Barnes, he'll do it and Barnes won't get a kick. He is the best player that we have in this country to mark the best striker in the world."

Fergie dropped Steve Bruce so that I should play in his place against Barcelona and although Steve did not agree with the decision, he took it well. I should explain that Romario of Brazil was just about the world's best player at the time and there were others in the Barcelona line-up, like Hristo Stoichkov, perfectly capable of winning a match on their own. Schmeichel and Cantona were therefore marooned in the stands at the Nou Camp as we were demolished 4-0 in front of a colossal crowd of 114,432. Our side was so short of class and quality that we were overwhelmed and Romario gave us a bit of a runaround, scoring once on the stroke of half-time and inflicted on us a thoroughly chastening night.

Soon after that, with the injury causing me increasing discomfort, it was decided I should have an operation and I think, from that moment, my career at Manchester United, as a front line performer, was over. I was recovering as United slid out at the earliest stage, collecting six points from six games by beating Gothenburg and Galatasaray (I'm pleased to say) but losing to Barcelona and to Gothenburg in the return. I actually started more European games than domestic matches that season but then came the dreaded operation.

I never properly recovered from this surgery, physically or mentally. The operation, thought to be straightforward enough, did not go well. There were unexpected complications because the ligaments in my ankle had been ruptured and it was clear that I faced a long lay-off. With the ankle immobilised in plaster for six weeks, my whole life threatened to disintegrate. I became crowded by negative thoughts about declining powers. Even when I attempted to come back, things had changed. I was training with the reserves when I was sent packing to hospital again, this time to remove a cartilage in my left knee.

Medical men told me that when part of the body is struggling, other parts tend to compensate and pressure develops where there had been previous injury. In this case, while my right ankle was causing problems, the left cartilage was bearing the brunt, so to speak. It was a thoroughly wretched time. I socialised more than I should have done, drank more than was good for me, and a dark depression set in. I don't excuse myself. I was close to Denis Irwin and he did what he could to raise my spirits, but in football you have to look after your own interests and you realise that it is hard to stay part of the inner circle when you cannot contribute. After that, you can become bad news.

Sir Alex also did his best to involve me in team talks and in other ways, but I must have looked like a pining dog, wandering around the Cliff looking sorry for myself. I felt I was missing out, excluded from the dressing room camaraderie by my injury and my continued absence and with no end to any of this in sight. My existence consisted of driving to the training ground for treatment with our physiotherapist, Dave Fevre, and leaving after all my pals had gone. There were dreary, silent days when the only people to be found at the Cliff were Dave, the boss, a gaggle of youngsters and me.

My marriage to Wendy was by then drawing to a close. Moving in the first place to Manchester lost me that marriage. We had met as teenagers and experienced a lot together but my moods did not help. Withdrawn and introverted, I admit I became a little bit selfish and I realised I wanted a change. Wendy gave me the chance to split up and I took it, no longer having to answer to anyone and, in the process of a breaking relationship, I am sorry to say it badly affected my daughter. Only now are Georgie and I close again.

I had everything anyone from my sort of background could possibly want and in rational moments I knew people would have paid good money to be able to do half of what I had done in football. But I was still not happy. I was living in an upmarket, four-bedroom house in Bramhall on the expensive southern fringes of Manchester, there was a gardener to cut the grass because I did not want to, and yet I was filled by pessimism and doubt.

In my isolation, I realised I should not have played those European matches, but there was no way I could let down Sir Alex, even though I was virtually playing on one effective leg and when, eventually, I did start to return to something resembling full fitness, I knew deep down I was not the player I had been at my best. My great playing assets seemed to have been stripped from me and left on the hospital floor. I could no longer turn or change direction as quickly as I had, my spring had seemingly deserted me and the talents which had made me special had disappeared. Or so I thought. Looking back, I think I psyched myself out, expecting to struggle and fail and then not being surprised when I did.

There is no doubt my body had changed because it can only take so many knocks before it compensates and alters. I walked differently, ran differently; it was simply not me any more. The longer I was away from the first team scene, the more, I am sure I came to be regarded by the hierarchy as dead wood. In my state, I was no good to the manager.

Without me, the team coped perfectly adequately but not with the level of achievement of the previous season, though that was a coincidence. We were runners-up in the league to Blackburn by a point and lost in the FA Cup Final to Everton, 1-0, tiny margins separating success and comparative failure. I watched at Wembley as the FA Cup slipped from our grasp, still feeling sad and helpless. At least the FA Cup Final signalled the end of the 1994/95 season, a year best forgotten for me and, for that matter, probably for Eric Cantona, our unpredictable genius of a player.

For all the many fantastic things he did for us at Manchester United, for all his stunning goals and inspirational performances, I fear Eric will be remembered principally for one spectacular incident at Crystal Palace when he drop-kicked a barracking spectator after being sent off. It was an extraordinary sight. I was there on the bench when Eric became involved in a fracas with Palace's Richard Shaw and was dismissed. It was a poor sending-off in my view but none of us was prepared for what happened next as he made his way along the side of the pitch to the dressing room. He told us later he was desperate to go to the toilet but that mattered little as he launched both feet at the fan for a full-blooded assault before being arrested by stunned policemen.

Eric was wrong and he knew it, and I am surprised he reacted in the way he did. What he endured in the way of baiting and hostility from the terraces that day, all black players endured every match throughout the 1980s. If I, and others like John Barnes had reacted, in the way Eric did, to every vicious comment from fans I would have ended up drop-kicking thousands. We became used to the mindless abuse and learned to ignore the nastiness and stupidity, but Eric had known only applause and adulation.

I must say that, having regretted his action, he took his punishment like a man. Faced with a community service order, Eric served his penalty with honour and distinction and genuinely enjoyed coaching children, which was his allotted task. There was a smile on his face as he went about his business and I think, punishment that it was, he got more out of it than he expected.

Meanwhile, I was still sulking and feeling bad about life. I suppose it might have helped if there had been a hobby or a busy life outside football to engross me and take me out of myself. Some footballers are gamblers. Bryan Robson, for instance, loved his racing, but I was not among them. Others liked their golf but, again, it was not for me. Sir Alex was a particularly enthusiastic golfer and was inclined to win if he cheated, but hacking out of a bunker did not appeal. I'm afraid my interests were rather more solitary. I stayed at home watching television or spent the afternoons wandering around the city centre shops. I am a restless soul and I need to be doing something all the time but perhaps it might have been better for me if there had been more to occupy me while I mulled over my injuries and their consequences.

At the start of the next season, 1995/96, my fifth as a Manchester United player, there was a further anxiety to consider. It was the last year of my contract and, by now, in my absence, a new team had begun to take shape. The young lads like Nicky Butt, who had once cleaned my boots, had taken my place in the team. Butt, the Nevilles, David Beckham and Paul Scholes had come bursting to the fore as the new face of Manchester United. There were, briefly, hopes, too, for other juniors like Chris Casper, Terry Cooke, John O'Kane, Ronnie Wallwork and Ben Thornley.

Robson, the driving force of a previous generation, had gone and Bruce, McClair, Pallister and myself were all the wrong side of 30 and inevitably set to follow one day. I just wanted my 'one day' to be later rather than sooner. At least I was fit, as fit anyway as I had been for a year or two, but Gary Neville was now wearing my coveted number two shirt and was playing well enough to suggest he had a big future as, of course, he had.

Gary was already a mature and dependable right-back and doing the job I once did with remarkable efficiency for one so young. My only hope of regaining a place in the team appeared to revolve around injuries to others – and I certainly did not want that – or that my versatility across the back four might open a gap. My expectations were raised when I was selected for the pre-season tour of Malaysia and was in the starting line-up for two matches in Kuala Lumpur against Selangor, which we won 4-1 and 2-0. It was so hot and humid in the stadium that some of us lost up to two litres of fluid on each occasion, and my improvement appeared to be confirmed when I played in four other friendlies at Birmingham, Bradford City, Shelbourne and East Fife in six hectic days.

My knee and other ailments stood up well and my optimism about the next season increased when Fergie experimented at East Fife with a five-man defence in which I had an integral role. On 19th August at Villa Park, the opening day of the Premiership season, imagine my delight and relief after all I had been through when my name was listed in our back five which also included Phil and Gary Neville, Irwin and Pallister. If we could make this work, then maybe this would be the blueprint for the whole season. It was vital, therefore, that we made a success of the new system in its first big test.

Villa on their own ground is always a difficult fixture and while the five-man defensive formula worked at East Fife, it was a different matter to subjugate the pace of Dwight Yorke, later a United icon, and the power of Savo Milosevic. To say we failed would be an understatement. We were three goals behind before we knew what had hit us. Ian Taylor, Mark Draper and a Yorke penalty left us trailing hopelessly by half-time and David Beckham's goal after coming on as a second half substitute was meagre consolation.

The five-man defence, on which I rested so many hopes, was dismantled on the spot, to be replaced by a conventional back four, and United went on to win eight and draw two of their next ten league matches, the experiment long since thrown in the dustbin. Unfortunately, it was me who was sacrificed when our defensive plans were returned to the drawing board. It's true I did not play well against Villa that day, but I don't think I was any worse than the others. So all

I could do was keep fit, keep improving and wait for another opportunity.

It came at home to Bolton less than a month later and it was simply wonderful to be back at Old Trafford on a match day, back in the old routine and back among the old dressing room banter. At QPR, my routine was inevitably dictated by the fact that I lived the other side of London. I left home at noon for a 3pm kick-off because I anticipated it would always take at least 90 minutes to negotiate the 26 congested miles from Billericay. At Manchester United, my preparation was altogether more leisurely. One of the benefits of having to travel a short distance and on freer roads was that I could stay in bed longer on a Saturday morning, watching the cartoons on television. Then I liked a cup of coffee before heading off to Old Trafford about two hours before the kick-off.

Once I had parked, signed an autograph or two, accepted the good wishes of supporters and got inside the stadium, it was time for a meal. My choice was either poached egg or chicken, depending on how we had done in our previous match. If we had won, it was a superstition of mine to eat what I had eaten then. Footballers are superstitious and that was mine. That September day before the Bolton match, it was as if all my troubles were at last behind me, but I knew that I was only playing because regular choice Gary Neville was absent and it was hard to shake off the impression that I was merely a stand-in. Even that was better than watching, with no chance of ever returning.

Bolton were no problem and we won 3-0 with two goals from Paul Scholes and another from Giggs and I was even more delighted when I retained my place for the next match, a goalless draw at Sheffield United. Gary Neville was again missing and I think I had every right to feel some sense of satisfaction at having been part of a defence which had not conceded a goal in two games. However, always at the back of my mind, was the feeling that once Gary was available again I would be the one to make way for him, and so it proved. To my intense disappointment, but not surprise, Gary was back for the home match with Liverpool and my brief flirtation with the limelight was extinguished before I had had the chance to bask in it again.

The longer I was out of the team, the worse it got. I found myself playing for the reserves in the Pontins League alongside many players who were never going to play in our Premiership side or youngsters so raw they had barely left school. At Manchester United, they take every league at every level incredibly seriously so there was no coasting for an old hand like me. I played in 12 of the 34 matches, staying as alert and as fit as I could, and yes, we did win the league and, no, I did not play enough to get a medal. At least I was playing and training every day but it was another three months, Boxing Day, before I was recalled to the defence at Leeds, who were always a tough proposition, at the start of the busy Christmas period.

I am afraid it did not work out as I had hoped and this was not my passport back into the side. I was replaced, by David May, and we fell away to a 3-1 defeat. I came on as a substitute against QPR on 30th December in a 2-1 win and then on New Year's Day 1996 I played my last match for Manchester United. I played at right-back at Tottenham, of all places, when we were thrashed 4-1 and it is fair to say I did not do myself any kind of justice. I was poor. I knew it and, more importantly, so did our manager.

The rest of the season just drifted away from me and I ended up playing more times in total in the reserves than in the first team. I had made one Coca-Cola Cup appearance in the humiliating 4-3 aggregate defeat by York City, another as a substitute in the Uefa Cup, and a couple in the FA Cup on the way to Wembley. We were playing at Elm Park, Reading, in the fourth round when I was sent on as a replacement. My first, clumsy, touch resulted in a yellow card from the referee Jeff Winter for a foul on Mick Gooding and my second resulted in a collector's item goal. I smashed a fierce angled cross-shot from the right wing towards the net and the Reading goalkeeper, Nicky Hammond, could only push it on to the inside of his near post on its way into the net. Was it a shot or a cross? To anyone who does not know me, it was a lovely sweeping shot to the keeper's right hand. To anyone who knows me, it was a cross.

Without me, United swept along to their second league and cup Double in three years. In the FA Cup they defeated Manchester City, Southampton and Chelsea after my starring role at Reading and then beat Liverpool 1-0 in the final at Wembley.

In the league, over the second half of the season from January, we lost only once, at Southampton, in 16 matches to finish top. In fact, we lost only six times in the Premiership in the whole of that season and I had the misfortune to play in three of those defeats. Eric Cantona, with 14 goals, confirmed his rehabilitation by becoming our top league scorer. I was little more than a spectator, a supporter almost, training every day and working as hard as I could but aware increasingly that my days at the world-famous Manchester United were coming to a close unless something unexpected happened.

Sadly, they were managing perfectly well in my absence. The young pretenders had now proved themselves completely capable of playing at this level, under the immense pressure that goes with being a Manchester United player, and were now on the verge of international careers. My day was done, and I realised that, at the very most, I might just get one more contract, perhaps for a year. The league and cup medals were dished out and shown off and none of them belonged to me. As the season ended in another round of celebrations I could not convincingly join, I went home expecting a call from the manager.

Looking on the plus side of my predicament, I was still only 32, was experienced and wise in the ways of

Manchester United and could drop into the team at right-back, central defender or sweeper. I was fit again and willing and the manager knew I would rather die than fail him. On the minus side, Gary Neville was playing brilliantly at right-back, Manchester United had moved on to new heights and there was no denying the fact that I was not the player I had been in my prime.

No doubt the same reasoning had occurred to Sir Alex. So it was with a heavy heart that I set off for Old Trafford when the summons finally came. I knew why he wanted to speak to me, but as the stadium loomed in front of me, I still hoped. One more year would be about right, I thought. Right for United and right for me. There was to be no reprieve. Sir Alex was as straight as he had been with me every day of my five years at the club. There was no one else in the room when he told me that, as I was running out of contract later in the summer, there would not be the offer of another one when it expired. He said he was sorry, and I knew he meant it, but the interests of Manchester United were paramount to him and there could be no other considerations.

Sir Alex said Gary Neville was now his number one right-back and there was plenty of cover for him. As his words came out, I could feel myself filling up but I was determined not to be so undignified as to cry in his presence. That would have been so humiliating. I said goodbye, we shook hands and I left the room as silently as I had entered it a few short minutes earlier. To this day, I have never got over that moment of rejection.

What was I to do? Let's face it, I may only have been 32, and a player of that age with an international pedigree might normally expect another three or four years in the game, but I was battle-scarred and no longer sure of myself. The lack of regular first team football had eroded my self-belief and I feared for the future. I got home, sat down and pondered my predicament. I was in love with Manchester, the club, the place, the adulation and the people, and now it had been snatched away from me. I had got together a whole set of new friends in the north and had a house and a lifestyle to show for a healthy pay packet. I did not want to leave all this and begin again in some other part of the country and yet, unless I got a similar deal elsewhere, I could not stay here either.

It was an emotional journey home and an emotional day or two as I attempted to come to terms with my new status as an ex-Manchester United player. Who would want me? What had I to offer any other club except my CV? There were calls of condolence and sympathy, as if I had suffered a bereavement, which in a way I had, while other callers wished me well for the future. I was numb for weeks, maybe months, since football was all I knew and Manchester United all I cared about. At least my pride was intact.

In more rational moments I knew I would not have wanted to take another year on sufferance or out of loyalty. Unless you were playing, Old Trafford could be a lonely place. As the summer set in, I sat at home mulling over the consequences, unable to get away from the fact that I was now part of Manchester United's past, as much as Best, Law, Charlton and the tragic Munich heroes were and yet without the same legendary status. Where was I to go next?

Chapter 11

From Marseille to Chelsea

THE SOUTHERN French port of Marseille is a long way in so many respects from Manchester but the people share a love of football and a deep pride in their club. Just when I was beginning to fear I might not find a decent alternative to United, I got a call from my agent Neil Ramsey to tell me that Marseille of the French First Division wanted to have a look at me.

Until then, my most likely destination was Derby County, newly promoted to the Premiership and managed by my old boss at Queens Park Rangers, Jim Smith. Jim felt my experience would benefit his squad and help them make the transition to the top level. We briefly talked terms and Jim, anxious to get on with his team-building, gave me until the end of June to make up my mind. But I liked the idea of Marseille, partly because the money was potentially good and partly because it gave me the chance of a fresh start well away from Old Trafford.

Jim's deadline came and went, I'm afraid, without me making a decision and I went down to Marseille to have a look at what they had to offer. Their coach wanted to meet me and he asked me to spend a few days training with them so that I could test my ankle. The language barrier aside – I speak no French – it all went surprisingly well. The ankle stood up to rigorous training sessions, I examined and liked the look of the club's stadium and then the coach sat me down to discuss where exactly I would be playing in his team and the sort of tactics he intended to employ. When it came to money, the amount offered was the same as I had been getting at Manchester United so it all seemed too good to be true.

Joel Cantona, brother of Eric, a man knowledgeable of French football, met me one day and said how much Marseille liked the prospect of signing me. All that appeared to remain was a detailed discussion on my contract and I would have been a Marseille player. Marseille and Manchester United were not unalike in that they had dominated their domestic competitions over the years. The record books showed that, at the time I was intending to join them, Marseille had won the league eight times and the cup on ten occasions, so there were historical similarities and expectations among supporters that suited me fine.

There was still no reaction from my ankle to the training sessions and I looked forward to completing the formalities of signing the forms. Then, without a hint of trouble and without a word of warning, I got a call from Ramsey. There was a problem. The coach was worried about my ankle. To say I was shocked was only the half of it because when I left Marseille there were handshakes all round and a general agreement that I would sign and move to France ready for business. I was really looking forward to it, getting away from Manchester where my divorce to Wendy was being finalised, and immersing myself in the whole Mediterranean experience. Suddenly it was all off.

Only later, sadly far too late, did I discover there had been a demand for an extra £50,000. Marseille, believing the terms were already perfectly adequate, would not comply, and told us the offer was no longer available. There should have been enough money to close the transfer and

I was mystified by the whole tortuous transaction. But the outcome was that there was no way I could now get back to Marseille and I had to start the process of finding a club nearer home. A dream move had evaporated in front of me for no reason that was obvious.

Had I accepted Jim Smith's offer by the end of June, as he had asked, I would have been sitting comfortably on a two-year contract at Derby but, when I got in touch belatedly, almost pleading for another chance, Jim said that deal had been withdrawn. The best he could organise for me was a trial and a four-week contract from the start of August with the Premiership season starting on the 17th. For a short time I had trained at Portsmouth where another former QPR man, Terry Fenwick, was manager, and I like to think it went well, but I preferred Derby because they were new to the Premiership and I relished the idea of the challenge. There was, in addition, just a vague inkling that I wanted to prove a few people at Old Trafford wrong by playing regularly again in the Premiership.

When all was said and done, it was the best offer open to me. Even so, it was strange playing at the old Baseball Ground in the white shirt of Derby although, at least in theory, the ram was now on my side. Jim obviously saw enough of me in pre-season training to put me straight into the team for the first fixture at home to Leeds where we recovered from a goal deficit at half-time to draw 3-3 in a top-class match. The debut-making Lee Bowyer was among the Leeds scorers and I appeared to make a decent first impression because Smith was quoted as saying "I intend to open negotiations to secure him permanently", but it never happened and I never really knew why he changed his mind.

In the next match, a 1-1 draw at Tottenham, I was substituted for Sean Flynn with five minutes to go and, after I had come off, Christian Dailly equalised in stoppage time. In the third, in the 2-0 defeat at Aston Villa, I played the whole 90 minutes. Jim decided to give me a total of three months to see if I could stay injury-free and to give him some cover in the hectic early-season schedule, which was some measure of security, but, just when everything seemed to be going smoothly, I hurt my back at the start of September and I think that was the beginning of the end for me there.

I recovered in time to be among the substitutes against Manchester United at the Baseball Ground on 4th September but I was denied the honour-satisfying chance to get into the action so my last involvement with Manchester United came and went quietly from the anonymity of the subs' bench. I have to say I don't remember speaking to Sir Alex that day, but it was good to see some of my old team-mates and remind them that I was alive and kicking (or kicking in the warm-up). The match was drawn 1-1, a creditable result for us against the champions and, for me, there was no conflict of loyalties.

My only other league start for Derby was against Sheffield Wednesday at Hillsborough on 21st September at right-back and, again, I thought I had made a full contribution to a goalless draw. I did play in two legs of a Coca-Cola Cup defeat by Luton, in the first of which I was booked by the young Graham Poll, and I have to say I don't think I played any worse than any other defender but it was not my opinion which counted.

Deep into my third month at Derby I was no longer getting a game and you didn't need to be a genius to realise that my time was running out. Steve McClaren, now England's assistant manager, was Jim's number two and I think that between them they felt I still had a problem with the ankle and had lost a little of my mobility. They were wary that I would break down again at some stage and be saddled with me on a longer-term agreement.

The problem was that I was living in a hotel in Derby, having cut my ties with Manchester, and I never felt settled.

The knock-on from this was that at Derby I swiftly formed the impression I was on permanent trial and, because of McClaren and Smith's lack of confidence in me, I became scared to make a mistake. I suppose I was therefore a little tentative and not as authoritative as a former England international of my background should have been. I knew I was for the chop at the end of the third month when Jim Smith, a man I greatly respected, called me over and told me he could not keep me on. I think he was as disappointed as I was.

Next stop Sheffield United and a change of hotel. Howard Kendall, the Sheffield manager, had shown interest in me when he was in charge of Everton and when I was at Queens Park Rangers, looking to leave Loftus Road. You will remember how I received racist threats from Everton fans when it looked as if I might move to Merseyside but, in any case, transfer talks never got very far.

In football, nothing stays the same for long and, five years down the line, Howard had also moved on, trying to breathe life into a potentially big club. From being a commodity as a current international at QPR, with a choice of top clubs to join, I was now a sort of wandering minstrel and, for all Sheffield United's aspirations and background, Howard was managing a club outside the Premiership. In both cases our pasts were more promising than our futures in football, but we each had to make the best of our predicaments.

I can't say I much enjoyed my three months at Bramall Lane and that's no disrespect to the club, the fans, Howard or my colleagues. I found it all very strange and, to be honest, not like anything I had experienced before. With the wonderful benefit of hindsight, I can see now that I was still recovering from being a Manchester United player, still getting over the shock of being cast adrift, rightly, by Sir Alex Ferguson. The problem was that I still thought of myself as a United player, albeit a displaced one, and I realise now that I was sulking, feeling that somehow I should not be there.

Where once I had Keane and Ince to receive my five-yard passes, I was now being advised to lump the ball 40 yards down the field to our big target man Gareth Taylor for him to bring Petr Katchuro and Andy Walker into play and, in fairness to Kendall, it was a tactic that often worked. Sheffield United finished fifth that season, narrowly missing a return to the Premiership. Nigel Spackman, another refugee from Loftus Road, was playing in midfield, giving me someone to relate to, but it was all so different to anything I had known.

Besides, while hitting the ball down the other end of the pitch may be second nature to many players in the lower divisions, I had been schooled at Fulham and Queens Park Rangers to keep the ball on the ground and play it simply. That, I believe, was one of the reasons Manchester United had bought me, because I was already playing in their style. I could not have struck the ball 40 yards even if I tried and certainly not with any accuracy because my leg muscles were not conditioned to the art of by-passing the midfield. I know Wimbledon were playing this way in the Premiership successfully, and to the annoyance of their expensive rivals, but it should be said in their defence that they possessed some high-class players who could have adapted to any method.

In retrospect, I should have got a grip of myself, and known better than to expect to find Manchester United replicated at Derby and Sheffield United. I should also have been a lot more positive because it was not necessarily the end of the world to be playing for such solid, honest clubs. They were good clubs with tremendous histories of their own and did not deserve my constant, unfair comparisons. Truth be told, I struggled over my ten appearances for Sheffield United, failing to adapt to my change in circumstances or to the more aggressive ethos of the First

Division and not doing myself or my reputation any justice. Stuck in yet another hotel, it was hard to feel I belonged to Sheffield United.

There was a big drinking culture among their players, without naming names, and that at least provided an escape of sorts and some fun, but I knew it could not last. My ten appearances in the red and white stripes included the first three at Port Vale, Bolton and Swindon as a substitute before making my full debut, incredibly, away to Queens Park Rangers where I was at right-back and we lost 1-0. It was strange going back not as a Manchester United player but there was a loyal cheer when my name was read out over the public address system and the welcome was as warm as it was when I wore the blue and white hoops with such pride.

I also played against Huddersfield, Portsmouth, Oxford, Palace, Barnsley and Bradford. The wins against Portsmouth (1-0) and Bradford (2-1) took us into second place but my own performances were by no means outstanding. Barnsley and Bradford, incidentally, were not my favourite grounds, nor any from Yorkshire, if I was to generalise. I am not sure why they should be any more hostile than other parts of England but none of the black players ever looked forward to playing in Yorkshire. There was no getting away from the fact that the Yorkies were always the worst in terms of racial abuse when I was starting out in the 1980s. Leeds were as bad, if not the worst of the lot, because the crowd size was bigger but, as the greater number of black players came into the game, the abuse diminished or was less evident.

I must say that players from Yorkshire clubs never gave me any extra trouble on the pitch with derogatory comments about my colour. It did happen, of course, elsewhere occasionally, although I cannot remember any specific examples, but my way of getting back at the perpetrators was to go to the black players among our opponents and tell them what their so-called team-mates had said about me and left it in their hands for retribution or admonishment.

Howard Kendall was to become the second top-class manager to discover that I was not the player they had expected me to be. Jim Smith was being polite when he said there was no room for me, Howard made many of the same noises about budgets, being well covered in defence and other well-meaning platitudes, but I got the message loud and clear. My attitude was not as good as it should have been and my performances on the pitch were not as professional or as committed as they should been from Paul Parker, formerly of Manchester United and England. My heart was simply not in it.

I could not complain or offer excuses, and there was no one to blame other than myself, although I was bound to think back to the Marseille incident and wonder. Derby and Sheffield United were great opportunities for me, one in the Premiership and the other trying to get into it, but I did not take them. As 1996 turned into 1997, I was out of a job and the future was decidedly bleak. I had a horrible fear that I may have reached the end of the football world.

But in my darkest hour who should step forward but Fulham, the riverside club where my career had first kicked off all those years ago. I still had plenty of friends down there in South West London and there was something reassuringly familiar about the old cottage in the corner of the ground, a sense of permanence in a much-changing world, much-changing for me, anyway.

When I had left Fulham the best part of a decade earlier, the club had been on its knees with its finances in a chaotic mess and the best players being sold just to survive. The club had slumped a long way to the Third Division by 1994 and, when I joined them three years later, here they were, playing teams like Hereford, Scarborough, Rochdale and Barnet as equals. For someone like me, a Fulham player from childhood, it had been hard to watch develop, even from the lofty heights of Manchester United. But there was change in the air, change for the better.

Mohamed Al-Fayed had become chairman and was starting to put his considerable fortune into the club and optimism had gradually begun to replace years of pessimism. Micky Adams was considered one of the bright young managers at the time and when I got a call from him in early January 1997, I was genuinely happy at the prospect of helping the club get promotion. They were handily placed at the halfway stage in the season with a real chance of going up and, although Adams could not offer me a contract as such, there was talk of something being on the table if all went well.

After what had happened at Derby and Sheffield United, I was just glad to be involved and agreed that it would be best for me to be paid on non-contract terms. That gave Fulham the chance to check my ankle and me the chance to see if rejoining my old club really was a good idea. Adams was a great enthusiast and initially he impressed with his fierce desire to get Fulham away from the league's lowest division and back on the path to reclaiming a proper place back among football's elite. It was going to be a long journey, recovering from the mistakes of the past, but it could be done.

Adams told me he wanted me to be sweeper behind the central defenders Mark Blake and Nick Cusack and that was not where I saw my future, the first indication that all might not be well. I had been used to playing right-back and of course I explained this to the manager, but he insisted I tried it on my first match back at Fulham, at home to Darlington on 11th January. When I left Fulham the first time, I was used to playing in front of crowds of double the 5,735 who turned up that day, although I don't suppose Darlington brought many fans down with them. What amazed me that day was the warm and wonderful reception I got from the Fulham supporters. It was quite touching because I had been away so long and I did not realise how popular I was, still, among them.

We coasted through that match 6-0 and when I was substituted I got another rousing round of applause as I left the pitch. The problem was that Adams had noticed it as well, and was not best pleased. I think he became jealous, seeing me not as a returning, conquering hero but as a threat. Adams knew I had been a popular player in the past but I don't think he expected me to be that popular. As a result, his attitude towards me changed overnight. All managers are wary in an insecure profession of bringing in, maybe unwittingly, somebody who might replace them down the line if a few results go against them. Not that I saw myself as a rival and I was very sackable, being on a match-to-match contract, but that was obviously not how he saw it.

We had to provide our own training kit and Adams began to waste no chance to put me down in front of his coaches, Alan Cork and John Marshall, and the playing staff. Marshall was reluctant to join in the banter at my expense because we had been team-mates in the past in my first spell at Fulham and we had always got on well. I played in the next match, a 2-1 defeat three days later at Colchester, but was then left out of the team for the next two fixtures against Torquay and Scunthorpe.

Then on Friday 31st January, I drove for two and a half hours around London from where I was now living in Essex to Fulham's training ground at Tolworth in Surrey for a light work-out in preparation for a match at home to Cardiff that night. It was a freezing day and I went out on to the training pitch in a pair of tracksuit bottoms, partly because of the cold and partly for the simple reason that I had no shorts. The club had never given me any.

Adams saw this as a personal affront. "You can't train," he shouted. "I'm the only one allowed to wear tracksuit bottoms at training. Who do you think you are?" This outburst came in front of all the other players and was, I think, a deliberate attempt to belittle me. It got worse even after he had calmed down. Adams said he wanted me to play as a wing-back, a position I had not occupied since playing for England in Italia 90, the best part of seven years before.

I tried explaining to him that I was not a wing-back, and Italy aside, never had been, but Adams had formulated his plans. We lost 4-1 after hanging around all day waiting to play in the evening, and it's fair to say I was not a success. I was substituted in the second half, and while there was applause again for me from our supporters, I had come to the conclusion it was all over, again. Bill Muddyman, Fulham's vice-chairman, wanted me to have a longer contract, until the end of the season at least, but I knew Adams was looking to get rid of me at the first available opportunity.

A few days later Adams called me into his office with Cork and a sheepish Marshall. Marshall could not look me in the eye because he knew what was coming. Adams duly told me that there was no room and no contract and that was the dismal, downbeat end of me and Fulham, my Fulham. I left the training ground bitter and sore having formed the firm impression that Adams had enjoyed bombing me out. While I could accept and respect the decisions made by someone like Sir Alex Ferguson, Jim Smith and Howard Kendall, it was another thing altogether being fired by Micky Adams.

I was living by now with Nicola, the mother later of my sons Jake and Max, and when I got home she could see I was upset and dejected, a beaten man. The season was six months old and I had been fired by three clubs already, four in nine months if United were included. From being a Manchester United player on a good salary and with an international reputation, I was now not even wanted by Third Division Fulham. I had dropped a long way in a very short time and my self-esteem had taken a dreadful knock.

Nicola put it all in perspective when she said: "What goes around, comes around." I am sure Adams would have justified his decision to send me packing by pointing to the league table at the end of the season. Fulham finished second and were promoted and, while I was delighted for the club, I was not that happy about Adams taking the credit.

Adams was later sacked by Al-Fayed and Nicola was proved right. None of which solved my immediate personal crisis. I had felt pretty low after Sheffield United had told me to go, though I could understand the thinking behind it, but it was much harder to be thrown out by Fulham. When you are no longer wanted by a club in the Third Division, the lowest rung, it usually means the end in football. Best to find a job outside the game.

What annoyed me, apart from Adams' behaviour, was the fact that I was not given a run in my best position at right-back. Sweeper and wing-back were no good to me. Here I was at not even 33, when many players are at their best, and although I felt I had something to offer football, football appeared to have nothing to offer me. Much as I cherished my medals and awards, there comes a time as unemployment looms when they don't mean very much. Not that I have ever considered selling them, or ever would.

I spent the whole of February 1997 without a club for the first time since I was a child, some 20 years. Nicola apart, who was I to turn to in my hour of need? Who was there to help me? For four long weeks I moped around the house, waiting for the phone to ring or trying to find myself yet another club. But there was no getting away from the facts. Three clubs had taken me in, in good faith, and been disappointed with what they had seen. The word may have got around that I was not the Paul Parker of old or that my ankle was still dodgy but I still felt I was capable of playing in the Premiership. The evidence – not wanted even by Third Division Fulham – appeared to contradict that, and as winter turned to spring, I had no idea what to do next. Then the phone rang. It was Chelsea.

This was an astonishing piece of luck, or so I thought, to get a club of Chelsea's standing when I was at my lowest ebb. Ruud Gullit was the manager and he was beginning the process of creating the foreign-based culture which was to follow in the Roman Abramovich era. Gianluca Vialli, Gianfranco Zola, Roberto Di Matteo and Franck Leboeuf were in place and making huge contributions to the revitalisation of the club. Mark Hughes, an integral part of the Manchester United success story, was still a major Premiership force. These were quality players, the sort to which I had been accustomed for the main part of my career, and now I was back among them.

Gwyn Williams, a prominent member of the Chelsea backroom staff as assistant manager, was the man behind my resuscitation. I had known Gwyn at Fulham and had always got on well with him. Gwyn was honest. He told me that Chelsea had key defenders injured or suspended and needed my experience as cover. There were no promises about the future, only that I was needed at Stamford Bridge until the end of the season. After that, there was no way of telling.

In signing for Chelsea, I became one of very few players to have appeared for all three West London clubs. It was all the more exciting because I was about to start work with the legendary, dreadlocked Ruud Gullit, an absolute superstar with the great Holland teams and with AC Milan. In the 1980s there was probably no bigger name in world football. But, as I was to discover, it was not so much Ruud Gullit as Rude Gullit.

171

Chapter 12

Ruud awakening

I WAS fortunate enough to play against Ruud Gullit for England against Holland and for Manchester United against AC Milan and there was no denying his excellence. Tall, fast, powerfully-built, brave, strong, brilliant in the air and fantastic on the ground, he was a defender's nightmare at his best. But I saw the other side of him. I saw Ruud Gullit, the weak and arrogant manager, a superstar who treated his players with dismissive disdain and a gross lack of courtesy. I came to despise him and not just for his ignorant behaviour to me.

I was fortunate in my time to come across some powerful characters as managers, people I respected even if they made decisions which went against my own interests. I understood that the team always came first and in that context their integrity and honesty was unquestioned. But Ruud Gullit brought a whole new dimension to the art of management. How not to do it.

For all his wonderful ability as a player, his basic problem was that he could not relate to players with lesser talent, which meant, therefore, that he could not understand most of them. It is often said that the best coaches were themselves moderate players and the reverse was true in Gullit's case. He was a brilliant player who could not comprehend the simple fact that not everyone was blessed with the sort of skills which came naturally to him.

The vast majority of us never knew what he wanted because he did not speak directly to us. Even at team meetings he could never get across his message, if there was one, and his tactics were never simple. I think in the end he just let superb players like Zola and Vialli get on with it, sent them out on to the pitch and hoped their great ability would prevail.

I would make allowances in my criticisms if Gullit struggled, as a foreigner, with the English language, but he spoke it perfectly well. Fundamentally I don't think he had much time for the English players, almost on principle. There were exceptions like Mark Hughes, if I may call him 'English', and Dennis Wise and one or two others, but overall I got the impression he did not like the way we played the beautiful game in this country. Perhaps he thought we were too aggressive, too unthinking, too much pace, not enough skill, I don't know.

But any manager has to know, as a basic part of his job, that only 11 can play on a given day, that only five can sit on the bench. It is how a manager treats and gets the best out of those not involved which decides a club's fate over a long season. Sir Alex never gave the cold shoulder to anyone. If you were out of the picture with him, he told you why. Jim Smith, Ray Harford, Don Howe – they all tried to get the best out of a whole squad because they were going to need the contribution of any number of players over 42 league games and nine long months. This, in my view, completely eluded Gullit. His man-management techniques were awful and he was without doubt the worst leader of a football club I have ever known.

Some people might think I was bitter because I was seen to be on the slide. If that was the case, I would admit to it now. But it was not just me he pretended did not exist. There were others who could testify to his brutal disregard for them. David Rocastle, an England international 14 times, was not even given a squad number. Mark Stein, holder of a Premiership record at one stage for scoring in the most successive matches, might just as well have been somewhere else and they never spoke. I heard later, also, how Rob Lee got the same treatment when Newcastle, for some reason, gave Gullit their manager's job. That was the way he did things. He surrounded himself with a little group of, mostly, foreign players and the rest of us could go to hell.

My mistake, if there was one, was being labelled a Gwyn Williams signing, not a Gullit choice. Gwyn saw me as a stop-gap, convinced his boss that I could help out for three or four months and, as a result, Gullit saw me like someone who had been sent by a temping agency. He never came over on my first day and welcomed me to the club, as most managers would, so I felt like a humble trainee virtually all the time I wore a blue Chelsea shirt. Williams and Gullit got on well enough, as far as I knew, but it was just that Gullit did not ever see me as his man.

My three months at Stamford Bridge must therefore go down as the least happy of my career and it got to the stage where I was driving along the M25 on my way to training when I became ensnarled for some 30 minutes in the sort of traffic which can make that particular motorway the most notorious in Britain. All the while I was stuck in three lanes of non-moving vehicles, I was mulling over my unhappy predicament at Chelsea. Eventually we reached junction 26, the Waltham Abbey turn-off, and I was still a long way from the Chelsea training ground on the other side of London. I suddenly thought to myself: "What am I doing here?" I got off the motorway, turned the car around and went home, later pleading illness. I was not enjoying myself and I knew then that my Chelsea career was going to be short-lived.

My first appearance was as a substitute for Andy Myers in the televised match with Sunderland at Stamford Bridge on 16th March. We were three goals ahead at one stage through Zola, Frank Sinclair and Dan Petrescu but Sunderland came back to make it 3-2 and my instructions were to steady the defence and prevent an equaliser. This I helped to do and two goals from Hughes and another from Di Matteo gave us an ultimately comfortable 6-2 win. Three days later I was again a substitute in a 1-0 home win over Southampton and a replacement again when we were beaten 1-0 at Middlesbrough, a result which left us sixth in the table and with any chance of the championship long since gone.

On 5th April 1997, the day after my 33rd birthday, I played in my 404th and last league match. After losing at Middlesbrough, Gullit decided I should start at Highbury and it was a sorry way to end my 16-year professional career. Ian Wright, David Platt and Dennis Bergkamp scored for Arsenal in a 3-0. I was one of three players replaced during the match and that was it, the end.

I still remained useful to Chelsea, not being cup-tied and, although the league form was patchy, we were at our best in the FA Cup, seeing off West Bromwich, Liverpool, Leicester after a replay, Portsmouth and then Wimbledon in the semi-final. This gave us a place in the final at Wembley against Middlesbrough and I wondered if I might finish my Chelsea career with an appearance at the wonderful old stadium.

None of us were any the wiser as to who was in and who was out, so 26 of us were required to report to Stamford Bridge on the day before the match to learn our fate. I had been given three tickets for the match to be distributed to friends and relations and I gave mine to Nicola and to Garry Hill, manager later at Dagenham and Weymouth, and his wife. I assumed, wrongly as it turned out, that even if I was not in the squad I would still get a seat, as a Chelsea player, somewhere in Wembley Stadium.

Not wanting to leave my car at Stamford Bridge if I was in the 18-man travelling party, I was obliged to head across London from Essex by the underground train, lugging behind me a huge bag of kit and covering my Chelsea tracksuit with a large coat as far as Fulham Broadway on the eve of one of the big matches in the domestic football calendar. When I got to the ground I discovered I was not in the squad, had not got a seat for the match and had not been invited to the post-match dinner at the Waldorf Hotel.

Those in Gullit's squad for the final were staying overnight at a hotel in Potters Bar, north of London, and on the day of the match I got a friend to drop me there. As the players, training staff, management and other sundry club servants boarded the bus to take them to Wembley Stadium, I hitched a ride. Unknown to them, I followed the other players on to the coach and sat down. It was the only way I could have got to the match. Best of all was the look on Gullit's face when he saw me chatting to the players as we made our way to Wembley. Talk about embarrassment. Once he spotted me, he refused to turn around again, staring ahead for the rest of the journey. He could not look me in the eye. I don't know what he expected me and the other six or seven unselected players to do. Go home and watch the match on television?

This unhappy saga was not over. Once at Wembley there was the little problem of getting into the stadium past security and I stood outside like an autograph hunter waiting to catch sight of some big names. I met another Chelsea outcast, Craig Burley, a Scottish international with more than a century of league appearances for the club, and another – I forget who – each of whom had played extensively that season but were not in the 18-man squad, outside and in a similar hapless position, namely not being able to get inside.

It was strange to think that Nicola and my friends were inside the ground getting ready to watch the match in comfort while I was outside looking as if I might have to resort to a ticket tout. At last we got a message to Adrian Titcombe, an FA official, and he was able to shepherd the three of us away from the throng and supplied us with tickets so that we could actually sit down. Chelsea then found it in the goodness of their hearts, having discovered us, to get us tickets for the players' area in the corporate hospitality section. Burley was so devastated by his original omission and then his humiliating treatment at Wembley that he did not bring himself to sit through the game and instead got stuck into the drink. Who could blame him?

Roberto Di Matteo scored the final's fastest goal in 43 seconds and Eddie Newton got another near the end so that Chelsea won 2-0. I joined the congratulations and was genuinely delighted for the Chelsea players, all of whom had been great to me from day one. I knew what it was like to win the FA Cup and I knew also how much it meant. It is one of the great moments in the life of any player. Even the great foreign imports, Zola, Vialli and others, were beaming with happiness. They had all welcomed me when I first joined the club and included me in any social occasions, so there was no question of me being in any way jealous or feeling left out among them and I shared their glory with enthusiasm. My grudge was against Gullit for excluding myself and the others so ruthlessly and, worse still, so neglectfully.

At least I had by now managed to blag a ticket for the Waldorf dinner. Jimmy Tarbuck and Kenny Lynch had been hired for the cabaret at no small expense but the night proved to be far from conventional and one I would not care to repeat. For a start, all the English black players were put together at the same table. I sat there with Michael Duberry, Newton and, I think, Rocastle and it must have looked odd to the many supporters who had somehow also managed to acquire tickets for what I thought would be a club-only celebratory night.

At Manchester United on a similar occasion, all the staff are invited, including all the box office staff and shop assistants, but not supporters. Some of our fans got drunk and the whole evening began to degenerate. After the dinner all the major players went off for a night out, something that again, would never have been allowed to happen at United. Wise, Hughes and Kevin Hitchcock, one of our goalkeepers, were alone in staying with us and, as the night wore on, not even the champagne could hide the fact that Chelsea and I were about to go our separate ways.

To my surprise, I was invited soon afterwards to join Chelsea on a tour to Thailand, which appeared to show they had not given up on me. But I had given up on them. The thought of working again with Gullit was too hard to bear and I rejected them. I told them I needed to find another club. They understood, and it was all over. At 33 I was finished as a professional footballer. In my opinion, Gullit had taken away from me what little had been left. The worst part was that I was not even that sad.

From Chelsea to Heybridge Swifts. Well, not quite. But to the outside world it might have looked that way. At the start of the 1997/98 season, I decided to take a step back from football. I didn't consider myself retired, as such, but after so many setbacks, I had grown tired of the game and became disillusioned. I'm afraid I was still blaming everyone else but myself for what had gone wrong over the past year.

There was no getting away from the fact that the previous season had been something of a disaster with four different clubs and cultures and 15 starts and, to be honest, I just could not stand the thought of going through all that again. I was fit and kept myself that way, though I'm not sure why, but I would be lying if I didn't admit to some pangs of envy as I thought how the Manchester United players would be assembling after a summer's break, ready for another tilt at all the game's big honours. Not much more than a year ago I was one of them. Now I was training alone and completely isolated, feeling as if I had fallen off the end of the world.

It's at low points in your life, like this was for me, that you find out who among the multitude of acquaintances you had met over the golden years can be counted as genuine friends. Tom South at Purfleet and Garry Hill, then manager of part-timers Heybridge Swifts, were proper pals and could see how I had become marooned on the fringes, with nothing to do, and tried to get me involved and boost my morale. Tom owned the non-league side Purfleet, a club near the Dartford Tunnel, and his team socialised at the Thurrock Hotel, which he also owned, next to their ground.

Purfleet, who are now known as Thurrock incidentally, played in the Ryman Premier and I used to have a drink with them on the odd occasion and I knew a few of the players. I had always liked the cut and thrust of the non-league game from my childhood days when I watched Dagenham and it always occurred to me that one day I might get involved at that level because essentially I loved football. Then Hill, a friend from 1985, asked me to train with Heybridge Swifts, also of the Ryman Premier. I played in some friendlies and in the Essex County Cup against Clacton but as the club embarked on a promising FA Cup run, which took them all the way through the qualifying rounds to the first round proper, it was always at the back of my mind that I did not want to get myself cup-tied, just in case I got a call from a full-time professional club. It was no more than a precaution, but I just wanted to keep my options open.

Heybridge did remarkably well and got through to the first round to earn a trip to Bournemouth. Garry wanted me to play but there was no way in a million years I was going to step in and take the place of someone who had helped Heybridge get that far. It got in the papers that I might be persuaded to play, which could have reminded one or two people in football that I was still around and without employment, but it was never on. I did travel with the team to Dean Court and watched them lose 3-0 after a brave enough fight, but it seemed odd to me, as I watched, that this should be the same competition I had won with Manchester United and only six months previously had endured the final as a Chelsea player. Here on the south coast on an autumn afternoon was what the FA Cup was really about, comparative giants and giant-killers, enthusiasm and determination, and people playing for the sheer joy of the game. What Ruud Gullit would have made of it, we will never discover.

I had a great day there and the Heybridge players, as a special treat, stayed overnight at a hotel in the town, and the fact that they had lost reasonably heavily made no difference to the way they partied and enjoyed their moment in the sun. I was happy for them, but I felt no inclination to join anyone, not because I felt I was above and beyond them, simply that I had lost my desire and drive to play competitive football. My ankle was causing me no trouble but my head and my lungs were all wrong. My head told me I did not want to get involved and my lungs were no longer those of a professional footballer. I was somehow removed from it all, despite Garry Hill's well-intentioned offer, and I thought it best at that moment to get out with my pride and reputation intact.

Using some money saved from my days at Manchester United, and, remember, I was just a few years too early before the gravy train pulled into professional football, I got involved in a vehicle leasing business in Brentwood, Essex, and it went well. Football was all I had ever known so this was a chance to find out about something else and, for a time, I genuinely enjoyed it, learning about how a company operated and the ways of business. I got a lot of work for the company from people who knew me as Paul Parker, the former footballer and, hard though it may be for people to understand, it was nice just not to be involved in football for a spell, to clear my mind, but I knew deep down it was not the real me.

While there was no denying how much I relished a different job and way of life, the truth was that I was missing football like hell, the great game was still nagging away at the back of my mind. All the people I knew as friends at United, some older than me, were still involved and playing in some instances. Denis Irwin was going strong; Gary Pallister and Steve Bruce, Paul Ince and Peter Schmeichel, they were all there somewhere in the public eye. Yet here I was, at 33, leasing cars for a living, football's forgotten man.

Part of me said stay out of football, change direction. Another part wanted me to keep trying. Alan Taylor, whose father had played a prominent role in my original discovery by Fulham, was manager of Farnborough Town in the Conference, the division below the Football League. He asked me down to training and I went in some trepidation without ever playing a game for them but then, from nowhere, Peter Reid, the manager at Sunderland, called to invite me for a trial in the north-east. This had to be my last chance, and I knew it.

Peter and I had been good friends at Queens Park Rangers and I think he was surprised that I was still unattached. There was no pressure from Peter. He just wanted to have a look to see if I had deteriorated beyond redemption while I needed to find out, once and for all, whether or not my last vestige of talent and know-how had deserted me. Top players like Niall Quinn and Kevin Phillips were banging in the goals as Sunderland attempted to get back into the Premiership after being relegated the previous season. They got preciously close, finishing in third place, but with no help from me, I'm afraid.

While it was pleasant to be training with professionals again, my competitive spirit had well and truly gone. Gone, I suspect, the day Sir Alex Ferguson showed me the Old Trafford exit door. Reidy did his best for me, thinking that I might provide just the sort of experience required to help a promotion campaign, but I fear we both knew the outcome of this trial before I was chosen to play in the reserves against Middlesbrough's second string at Durham City. Within minutes I sustained a groin injury and on any other day I would have come off. But the desire to prove to myself that I still had the right to call myself a professional footballer and my foolish pride refused me the right to surrender.

My stubbornness, my ego, call it what you will, forced me to stay on for the full 90 minutes. So inflamed was my groin, I could run only with pain and, yet again, I had not done myself proper justice. Reidy, who was doing a great job at Sunderland, did not need to tell me. I was on my way home. Sunderland, in any case, was too cold for a black man, but on the long journey back to Essex, more seriously, I did have the satisfaction of knowing that I had killed off my demons. I was now happy to accept that I could never again play at a full-time level. I was not dejected. I was not upset. It was a fact of life.

For the rest of that season and the whole of the next, I immersed myself in my leasing business, not wanting anything to do with football or footballers and believing that I would never again be involved in any way at any level. Of course it did not help my transition from footballer to businessman to see contemporaries on television, but it was no longer part of the world I inhabited.

It might have been that way even now had I not received a call from George Wakeling, manager of Dr Marten's League side Ashford Town in the summer of 1999. George wanted me to take over his job and become manager but I felt this was far too early. I became, instead, director of football, a rather grand title for a small club watched at home by no more than 300 people. I must say the spark was instantly rekindled and all my well-rehearsed opposition to returning to football melted before his call of invitation had been completed.

What I was about to find out the hard way was just how difficult life can be in the part-time game. The players have other jobs, which take priority, the turnstiles go rusty with under-use and there are always property-developing chairmen and club owners who see the little stadiums, often sited in town centres, as potentially nice little earners. Ashford in Kent meant a round trip of 150 miles for me from Billericay two or three times a week. Ashford was a post-war new town and had no footballing background or history and struggled by on a wing and a prayer. As with all such clubs, they were kept in business by a gaggle of well-meaning fans who manned the bars, painted the stands, produced the programmes and held fund-raisers to help pay the wages of not-very-good players. Ashford were in the throes of a takeover by a consortium which included the former England footballer Rodney Marsh, but in my brief dealings with him, a fat load of use he was to anyone.

The lovely little ground was perfectly positioned for development and, as the rudest possible introduction to football in the raw, George and I went months without payment while a battle for control was carried out behind us. We were threatened and told we would be harmed once we had inevitably been dismissed and took our cases to an employment tribunal. But we were not going to be intimidated and were awarded damages and back pay amounting to £26,000. That little episode was a bit of an eye-opener. I had no idea feelings could run so high but money was involved, and that said it all, really.

As war raged at Ashford, I got a job nearer home at Chelmsford as assistant manager to Gary Bellamy but not before I played in one, very emotional last match at Old Trafford in October 1999 in a testimonial for Sir Alex. I was honoured even to be selected as United took on the Rest of the World. I managed 20 minutes at right-back and there were three number sevens in Robson, Cantona and Beckham, all of us paying homage to one of the greatest managers of all time.

Old Trafford with 55,000 people inside is an awesome sight and there was no denying a tingle went down the spine, running out on to that famous pitch again. Fergie always said the 1994 team was his best ever and it was good to see so many old team-mates again in such a carefree atmosphere. There was a fabulous dinner afterwards at the GMX Centre as we relived great and not-so great moments. That fateful trip to Galatasaray was sure to have been mentioned. We had shared so much and seen so much, our lives having been defined by being Manchester United players, and it was hard to say goodbye. Sir Alex is good to those who have served him well and, every year, pride of place on my mantelpiece goes to his Christmas card.

Chelmsford, of course, would be happy to get 55,000 a year through their turnstiles but I was happy to link up with them in April 2000 after a chat with Bellamy, a former Wolves and Leyton Orient defender, and Peter Stroud, the chairman, who I had known for some time. Chelmsford may be a large commuter town, but the club had no ground of their own at the time and were playing in Billericay, not far from where I lived. I would go and watch them if I was free, so this was a great opportunity for me.

Bellamy was a quiet man, who liked his football played in the correct way with players attempting to pass to each other rather than hack it down the pitch, and he was shocked, I remember, to find out I had no job. By now I had parted from the vehicle leasing company and was in a sort of limbo, so that I needed to make a living once again from football. Stroud was a good guy and Bellamy well regarded in these circles, and we were promoted to the Dr Marten's League Premier Division at the end of the 2000/01 season.

Bellamy left in June 2001 and Stroud asked me to be Chelmsford's manager. I had enjoyed my coaching role and I was not at all sure I wanted the responsibility of being number one. I didn't see myself as Essex's answer to Sir Alex Ferguson but Stroud, who put a lot of time, effort and money into the club, was adamant: "If you don't take it, I will see you as a s**t-out merchant." I knew what he meant. Step forward the new boss of Chelmsford City.

It was a pleasure once I got used to the idea. Chelmsford were the biggest non-league side in the county and had survived years of ground-sharing with Billericay. They were my local team and I was proud to be in charge and I got involved from the first moment with a determination and desire to succeed which surprised even me. Had you opened the boot of my car at any time over the next couple of years you would have seen two bags of balls, bibs and cones, making it about as far removed from Manchester United as it was possible to be. And I loved every minute.

The Dr Marten's Premier Division would then have been about the sixth domestic level of football so there were some good teams and good players, many of them having played a decent grade or two higher. There were budgets to consider, signings to make, wages to pay and then, of course, there were balls, cones and bibs to collect at the end of frosty evenings on the training pitch. We had long journeys to Stafford, Weymouth, Newport (South Wales), Newport (Isle of Wight) and Tiverton, our bus picking up players on street corners and pubs at fringe towns and suburbs of London.

On Stroud's insistence, all the players wore club tie and blazer in an effort to invoke some belief in the club, but it was hard work. Some of the guys had come straight from daytime jobs, for others this was the only source of income, there was no chance to coach, only to assemble a side capable of not losing. That season we won 13 of our 42 league games and stayed up by two points, an achievement in itself after the way I had pleaded with and begged players even to train with us on a regular basis.

I suppose opposition fans saw me as a bit of a personality in that only four or five years earlier I had been playing on the big stage and while there was the occasional racist shout from the under-populated terraces away from Chelmsford, the stick I got was for being associated with Manchester United. For every fan who loves United, there is another who hates them. As crowds anywhere seldom exceeded 500, there was one thing I knew for certain, as I sat out in the rain in bleak footballing outposts, and that was there was no way I could ever be a Football League manager. I was already experiencing sleepless nights.

At the start of my second season in charge, 2002/03, I splashed out in financial terms on Phil Gray, a striker with a tremendous pedigree which included caps for Northern Ireland and high level stints at Sunderland and Luton. I reckon we were paying him £250 a week but he was a decent lad and keen. But he was too good for us. His hold-up play and thinking was far ahead of the average player and he began to become frustrated, losing his rag if a player of lesser ability failed to respond in the way he should have done. It was clear he would have to leave us for his own sake and for the sake of team morale and after a chat that's what happened and, in its way, it summed up the whole problem of non-league football.

Coming from my background and Gray's, our expectations were beyond the reality of the situation in which we found ourselves. For all that, we had a good season. Chelmsford finished ninth, a big improvement on the previous year, and won the Essex County Cup, beating Southend and Canvey Island on the way to the final where we defeated Aveley 5-0. I was looking forward to building a team for the following season, but then it all went horribly wrong. So, too, did a strange episode at Tottenham, the club of my childhood.

Chapter 13

Baby-sitting at Tottenham

I HAVE a strong affection for Fulham, Queens Park Rangers and, of course, Manchester United, but a true football fan never forgets his first terrace love. In my case, that meant Tottenham Hotspur.

I was a whisker away from becoming a Tottenham player until Maurice Watkins' fateful call to the Royal Lancaster Hotel and, had I signed, I would have been greatly honoured. I played numerous times against Tottenham over the course of my career and, as a professional, all youthful loyalties were forgotten.

Spurs became, in my mind, just another opponent to be beaten, but there was that magical moment when I actually got on the score-sheet against them for United in January 1993.

About 15 years earlier I would have been horrified had Manchester United put a goal past my beloved Tottenham and now, here I was, celebrating in front of the United fans, arms aloft, punching the air with unbridled happiness. Brian McClair and Ryan Giggs jumped all over me and I ran back down the pitch with a huge grin. I scored so infrequently that, when I did, it was a talking point in the United dressing room for weeks. I made sure of that. Did I have any regret at inflicting one of my rare goals on Spurs? Not in the least. I knew who paid my wages.

Deep into retirement, I got a call one day late in 2000 from John Moncur, Tottenham's youth development officer and father of the former West Ham player of the same name. Paul Allen, who had played for Spurs and West Ham, had resigned as coach to the Spurs Under-15s and Moncur suggested I might like to replace him on a part-time basis. Working with Chelmsford, it fitted in nicely, helped fill up my diary and I was grateful for the opportunity. Now that I was no longer involved in the full-time professional game, Spurs had become my local team again, in all senses, and the training ground at Chigwell was no more than 40 minutes away. I rather liked the idea of becoming Paul Parker of Tottenham, albeit about ten years late.

But what should have been a top job, grooming the Premiership stars of the future, and perhaps leading to a staff coaching appointment, was a major disappointment. I don't blame John Moncur because the system he had put in place was impeccably prepared and developed. I blame the parents. They wanted their kids to succeed more than the boys did themselves. Some of the lads, supposedly the cream of their generation in and around North London, did not want to be there. Anywhere but, in fact.

Maybe I was being naive, but I thought that any boy playing for the Under-15s side of a team of Tottenham's stature was, by definition, high-class and that they were all chasing the dream I chased at their age. In theory, they were a year away from being offered contracts as trainees with one of the biggest clubs in England, but you would never have known it either in terms of their ability or their attitude.

When I was a kid, playing football was all I ever wanted to do in life. There was no viable alternative. But instead of being confronted by a gaggle of eager youths, desperate to impress, I found myself in charge of a glorified baby-sitting service. The academy system should ensure that the best boys are filtered out from the age of nine, so that by 15 I should have been teacher, tutor and mentor to a group of kids with a real chance of becoming professional footballers. I feel certain I am right in saying, several years on, that only one of the boys I coached, Michael Malcolm (although Philip Ifill was in the year below), went on to sign a professional contract and if that was my fault, I would say so. I really believe it was not.

There were boys so obviously not up to standard that they were wasting their time and Tottenham's money and there were others who would rather have been tucked up at home in bed on a Sunday morning when we had matches against other academy sides. The trouble was that the parents appeared to me to get more out of it than their kids. They enjoyed the kudos of being able to say their boys were on Tottenham's books and they stood on the touchline in their Spurs jackets and replica shirts, pointing, shouting and whistling as if they were in the technical area at White Hart Lane in the heat of a Premiership game.

Other parents were far less involved. One dad used to drop his boy at the training ground and go off to the pub, returning half an hour after we had finished to pick him up. From day one, I could see with a trained eye that most of them were never going to play for a living and the rest, while not quite as useless, were unlikely to be good enough either. But it was another thing telling parents their little boy was not going to be the next Wayne Rooney. For any child to have left the club, a parent had to sign a registration cancellation form and, believe me, none of them were ever going to do that voluntarily. That would have almost certainly meant the end of the line and who was I to help administer the death blow?

Parents, not unreasonably, asked me what I thought of their kid and what was I supposed to say? I knew the vast majority were hopeless but I could not say the truth without offending, so it was easier to pass the buck and tell them to discuss the issue with Moncur or other members of the full-time coaching staff. When it came to matches I had to select a starting 11 and that invariably upset the parents of those not chosen. I felt we had to put out our best players, a decision which inevitably consigned a huge number of disappointed kids to the touchline.

Most of my time, up to 90 minutes at the end of each evening or Sunday morning, was spent discussing the pros and cons of boys with their increasingly anxious mothers and fathers. They heard only what they wanted to hear, so if I found something nice to say, they would latch on to it, as if I had given them a seal of approval. I wish I could have said what I really felt because in the long run it would have been kinder but, in effect, I was only delaying a nasty decision.

Not being empowered to say anything, I coached as best I could, but it was an impossible task, draining, dispiriting and, in some ways living a sort of lie. The worst part was that if parents were getting bad vibes about their precious offspring from me, they would question my judgement behind my back, turning the kids against me. This made it difficult to work, to attempt to improve the skills of those children who might one day at least be able to enjoy the game socially. Ideally, parents should have handed over responsibility to the club and stayed away to let us work, but that was never going to be the way. At first it was fun, but at the end of my only season with Spurs it had become the equivalent of a job to help pay the bills, boring but necessary.

I thought at the start it would be a way into the club I had supported as a boy although I soon came to the conclusion I was better off at Chelmsford. It would have helped had there been any kind of rapport with the other coaches but I am convinced they felt threatened by my presence as an ex-Manchester United player. Occasionally there were full-time vacancies at Tottenham and some of the other age-group coaches thought I was in pole position to get a staff placement because of my background with United and England.

They need not have fretted because I had made up my mind quite early that it was not something to interest me. The mere fact that I was an outsider, dare I say, a distinguished outsider, worked against me and I discovered a lot of bitterness directed towards me, I think, for not being like them, Tottenham through and through. Maybe it was jealousy, maybe they did not like my honesty, but ultimately I did not need a job that badly. I was glad to leave.

I formed the impression that my Manchester United connections were conspiring against me at Tottenham's Christmas dinner party in December 2000. All the coaching staff, to include those who, like me, ran the age groups as part-timers, were invited in an effort to make them feel part of the grand scheme of life at White Hart Lane. All the first team players were there. It was good public relations but my celebrity caused problems, rather than open doors.

As soon as Nicola and I got to the party, George Graham, the manager and inevitably the main man, came over and we became involved in intense discussions for up to half an hour. George did so for a purpose. I feel sure he saw me as different from the Spurs people who surrounded him. He asked questions and I gave him answers he could respect. He said I was a breath of fresh air. I think George was, deep down, an Arsenal man and, in me, he felt an affinity because I was someone also from outside the secluded environment of White Hart Lane.

David Pleat, his assistant, and a lovely guy, also came over to where we were sitting and introduced me to Sergei Rebrov, the Ukrainian striker, and spoke glowingly of me to him. My unsolicited, special treatment was noticed by the other youth coaches who had come to regard me as a rival. Nicola watched them watching me. She said: "They have been giving you dirty looks. There must be daggers in your back."

At least at Chelmsford I was dealing with adults who had no pretensions of grandeur. None of them were ever going to play for Spurs, but I enjoyed being their manager and 2002/03 was straightforward and enjoyable until March when our chairman and benefactor Peter Stroud, who had pumped £300,000 into the club in five years, resigned and the pressure fell immediately on me as his appointment. Trevor Wright, who had been joint chairman with Stroud, assumed control and from the moment he took over it was clear my position as manager was no longer safe.

Wright said all the right things, telling me I was not in any danger, but I did not believe him. I think he wanted a puppet manager, someone he could dictate to, but that was not my style. Sometimes he would talk at me for up to three hours and underneath it all I had a horrible feeling he wanted to take the club backwards. My fears were confirmed when I heard a rumour that he had told one of my staff that he was not going to pay my summer wages. Increasingly it dawned on me that, out of respect for Stroud, I knew I would eventually have to walk away. The timing was all-important.

As I said, we had a measure of success that year. Ninth was not bad and the Essex Cup success should have counted for something. My last match in charge was at Newport County on the final day of the season in May. On the way to South Wales on the team bus, the chairman asked me if I was leaving. I said nothing, although I had been tipped off that he had already offered my job to Steve Mosely of Aveley behind my back. Wright was not happy with the fact that our players were not wearing club blazers and ties, as a means of making a point to me, but I explained that since it was the last match of the season I had collected the blazers and stored them away for safe-keeping. After all who knew which players would still be at the club for the following season?

We won 5-1 and Wright kept us waiting on the coach, because he could, while he stayed drinking in the bar for almost an hour. Eventually he got on board and sat at the front. I made my way forward and told him: "You are getting what you want. I am resigning."

The journey was the better for having got it off my chest, but when we got to a stop-off point at Brentwood our defender Brian Statham, who had appeared for Brentford and Reading, got out of the side door in pursuit of another, Keith Sharman, who owed us a player-imposed 'fine' of £20 because he was not going out drinking with us that night. The chairman accused him of holding us up and Statham, perfectly politely, pointed out that any delay had been caused by him. After the chairman had got off, we all went for a great night out in Chelmsford.

The next evening was our player of the year awards and Wright warned me not to take any of the players with me, wherever I might be heading. I said: "They play for me, not the club." After I had gone to Welling a week or two later, I did indeed take three or four with me. Wright got nervous and, later in the summer, he spotted one of my likely targets in the Chelmsford streets. He told him I was a useless manager and, I am given to understand, said: "Why do you want to play for that black c**t?". With that, he told the player, who should remain anonymous, to follow him to the cashpoint so he could get him a signing-on fee.

But it was a shame. Chelmsford had enjoyed their best season for years and one man had ruined it. Trevor Wright either did not like me as a manager or maybe it was the colour of my skin which upset him. I will never know for certain. Mosely duly got my job and Wright gave him a heap of money to spend, much more than I had been allowed. But when the leagues were reorganised, Chelmsford failed to make the cut to get in to an elevated division named Conference South and Wright was eventually booted out.

I can't say I got any solace from that. I had built up a great affection for the club and I am pleased to report that Chelmsford have since gone home to a stadium of their own and are getting the sizeable crowds they deserve. The tragedy is that, after years of playing elsewhere and all the financial implications that go with being displaced, the town missed out on having a top-class non-league team for far too long.

From a personal point of view, having to resign was a setback. I can honestly say that managing Chelmsford was the only time I recovered any kind of enthusiasm for football from the fateful day Manchester United booted me out. Chelmsford had been a big club in the 1960s and 1970s and were my Essex team. I respected them and what they represented and, in other circumstances, I would have been happy to stay.

In the same month, May 2003, I was appointed manager of Chelmsford's Dr Marten's League Premier Division rivals, Welling United. The word got round the non-league circuit that I had left Chelmsford for budgetary reasons. But I, of course, knew differently. I wish I could say life was easier at Welling, but familiar problems – lack of money, lack of support – beset them.

Welling is just the other side of the River Thames from Purfleet, near the Dartford Tunnel and more London than suburban Kent. All they had going for them was one of the best pitches outside the Premiership, which they had to share with Erith and Belvedere for money reasons, and the usual small, patient, undemanding support. Otherwise it was a constant struggle to make ends meet. The fan base was not as solid as Chelmsford's because of the proximity of so many big clubs, and Kent hardly ever produces any players of note.

I don't think I was as committed as I should have been either. I suppose what had happened at Chelmsford knocked my confidence a little but the first season went well enough. We finished ninth, well ahead of Chelmsford in 18th, but I could sense my enthusiasm waning. Unlike Chelmsford, we did make the cut for Conference South, but by December 2004 I was rapidly losing my way. I can't blame boardroom pressure or the demands of a dictator. I'd had enough. I told them I wanted to get out and made it easy for them to sack me. I did not take it personally when they did.

I imagine some people will be wondering why I 'stooped' to the level of teams like Chelmsford and Welling, but I just love football. It is intrinsic to my soul. I like other sports and admire those who are good at what they do but I could watch football all day long if I can no longer play it meaningfully. I know of footballers who lost all interest in the game once they stopped and there were others who casually gave the impression of not even enjoying playing it.

I even turned out in the Chelmsford Sunday League when Garry Hill was manager of Priory Sports alongside ex-pros like Micky Droy and Alan Brazil and I was glad to be playing – the smell of Deep Heat is the same in any dressing room – and never for one moment did I think it was beneath my dignity. It was fun, and I hope I never lose that sense of enjoyment that I still get from the game. Even after I had left Welling I helped out a friend, Neil Cugley, at Folkestone Invicta for a short time in 2005, before my other commitments got in the way and, while it seems unlikely that I will ever return to management, nothing can ever be ruled out.

I should have saved more money when I was at the height of my earning power at Manchester United, but I frittered it away on cars, which have always fascinated me, and a hectic social life. I should have realised it was not going to last for ever, but when you are young and fit you don't think further than the next happy day. A divorce did nothing for my bank balance, either.

I would be lying if I said I did not envy the present players their colossal pay packets and in that respect I was born about ten years too early. None of us in my playing days, even the best, earned anything like the sort of money an average Premiership player can command today. I hope, for their sakes, it does not all end in tears one day, but, had I been playing now as a Manchester United player for the same five-year spell, I would have been set for life.

Not that I have any deep complaints about the way my life has turned out. I wish I had seen more of my daughter Georgie growing up in Reading where she and Wendy went after our divorce. I don't feel good about what happened and she resented me for a few years before I was able to make it up to her. I see her now when I am able, and we speak often on the phone but, what I can say is, I never lied to her. Even so, it's fair to say a sense of guilt remains on my part and I feel I owe her far more than I have so far been able to give.

I am with Nicola now and we have two children, Jake who is nine and six-year-old Max. I met Nicola in about 1995 when she was a buyer with Miss Selfridge and we live happily in a four-bedroom detached house in Billericay, not far from our respective parents and families. I cannot ever see us moving from that area, which makes us Essex people and proud of it.

But I still retain a deep affection for Manchester and the people of the north. I found them to be so open and friendly and they took to me from the moment I first moved to Cheshire. Part of me would like to live there even now and I am fortunate that I still get the chance to go back regularly to work at Old Trafford for MUTV, the club's own television station, as a pundit and analyser. As such, I am still on Manchester United's payroll, still involved in the club's affairs as an armchair fan and part of the Old Trafford core.

On the day of each match I make my way up the motorways from Billericay to our studios at Old Trafford, whether United are at home or away. It is strange, driving close to White Hart Lane or Highbury on a match day and spotting United fans heading that way when I am going in the opposite direction, northwards to a studio in an empty stadium. But it's part of a job I have grown to relish now and I no longer feel as nervous as I did when I started.

Lou Macari, Lee Martin, David May, Denis Irwin and Clayton Blackmore are among the other opinion-givers, Steve Bower is an excellent commentator and presenter alongside United legend Paddy Crerand and it is all brought together under the tight control of our producer, Mark Pearson. We are all glad to be part of the Manchester United family.

I hope I make a decent contribution on MUTV. I know a lot about the club and plenty about football at all levels and the difference between our station and others covering matches is that we are essentially United fans. It is in our blood. Our devotion to the club is reciprocated. There is a thriving ex-players' association, run by David Sadler from the Best-Law-Charlton period in the club's history, and our dinners are keenly anticipated. We all feel as involved as if we still ran out on to the pitch in the famous red shirts.

Four or five years ago I would not have been able to write this book. I was still quite bitter about the way my career had fallen away and I was consumed by self-pity. But a certain distance from what happened has given me the chance to view it all with the perspective retirement brings. I played with and against some of the greatest footballers in the world. Some deserved their reputation, some did not.

My most difficult opponent was the prolific-scoring Ian Rush of Liverpool, Leeds and Wales. Rush used to walk alongside you in the middle of a match, talking to you about how the game was going, a refereeing decision, anything. At first I was suspicious, thinking he was trying to wind me up, but after a few years I came to realise it was just his way. There was no malice, no nasty words, just the sort of banter you might expect on a Sunday morning parks pitch. But the affable countenance belied a ruthless nature in front of goal, as his fantastic scoring record proved. What made him especially difficult was his great acceleration over a short distance, a terrific turn of pace which tested every defender, even me at my quickest.

As a Manchester United player, it became hard to judge many players because opponents were so defensively inclined against us, home and away. But one who always caused me problems, and this might be a surprise, was Rick Holden, a scruffy, awkward left-winger with Oldham when they were in the Premiership. Holden never looked the part. He had no natural pace, was never going to beat me for basic speed and he could give the impression he was not interested. But he was a canny operator, hugging the touchline and was a great crosser of the ball. He had this way of getting his foot around the ball and propelling his cross with great accuracy just when you thought you had nailed him. In my opinion, he was a much underestimated player.

Clive Walker, briefly a team-mate at Loftus Road, always caused me problems with his pace and skill in his last three years at Brighton. Then there was Kenny Dalglish who had this habit of sticking his backside into you to make room and space for himself. The Liverpool striker was a magician and I had too much respect for him.

The hardest player was undoubtedly Bryan Robson. There was a presence about him, a ruthlessness, which instilled massive confidence in the rest of the team. Bryan left a trail of destruction like Muhammad Ali and, with him thundering through the middle of the pitch, you felt you could not lose. When he led the team out on to the pitch, his whole demeanour indicated that losing was not an option. Even after injuries had taken a wretched toll, there was no change in his attitude. Roy Keane, Paul Ince and Steve Bruce were all fearless, but Bryan was the bravest of them all.

There were some people we all hated. Mick Kennedy, an Irish international midfield player at places like Middlesbrough, Huddersfield, Portsmouth and Luton, was distinctly unpleasant, kicking opponents and spitting, while

Vinnie Jones singled out players he wanted to bully. They were invariably smaller. Sly kicks and verbals, he knew all the tricks.

Bullies can be cowards, but you would never have dared call big Billy Whitehurst a coward. Billy was a formidable, fearsome centre forward of the old belligerent style at Newcastle, Sunderland, Oxford and Reading, among many. No one messed with big Billy, except me. I was playing for Fulham against his Hull in November, 1985 and I must have kicked him accidentally, but that was not the way he saw it and swung a leg at me. We ended in a heap after a tackle and he sat on my chest. "Don't come near me again, you black t**t," he said. I could see the anger and threat in his eyes and knew he meant what he said. I promptly moved into midfield. We lost 5-0 and Billy scored.

Later, when he was running a pub in Sheffield (he supported Sheffield United), I reminded Billy of the incident and told him how I had been so scared of him that I had fled into midfield, dreading he might catch up with me. "I would have had to sneak up on you because I was never going to catch you," he was honest enough to admit.

Ian Wright of Crystal Palace and Arsenal was the most miserable centre forward there ever was. He moaned about every refereeing decision, even some that went for him, and once pushed and punched me off the ball because I was having a good game against him. Wright also had a big bust-up with Bruce, but that was Ian Wright. He was the loudest, loveliest bloke imaginable, always in your face, always trying to get under your skin – and often succeeding. He needed to shout, scream and harass everyone to get himself going. Off the pitch, everybody liked him. I also rated him highly as a striker because he could make a goal out of nothing, through his own work.

Gary Lineker, in my era, and Michael Owen needed the contribution of others to be successful. Lineker and Owen will go down as great scorers, but they did not have

Wright's ability to make his own luck. His Arsenal team-mate, Martin Keown, was an unpopular opponent. There was no disputing his effectiveness or his defensive ability, but he enjoyed kicking those he was marking and there was a cynicism about him. He knew what he was doing.

Danny Wallace was just about the unluckiest player in my time. Danny was a small London boy like me and we enjoyed some great tussles when he was a winger at Southampton. Later we were colleagues for England Under-21s and Manchester United, but Danny became ill with multiple sclerosis and was never able to fulfil his talent, one of the great tragedies of my playing time and a reminder that nothing can be taken for granted. I was honoured to play in his testimonial at St Mary's, Southampton, and it was sad that the Sky TV cameras should prefer to cover Keown's testimonial on the same night.

I didn't have many problems with referees although, had I been playing in today's less physical environment, I think I would have collected many more yellow and, therefore, red cards than I did. The best ref of my era was Roger Milford from Bristol. Roger was a bit of a poseur in many ways with his hot-pants style of short shorts but if you swore at him in the heat of the moment he would give as good as he got. He would talk to players throughout the game and earned our respect in a way that would probably not be possible at the present time.

I feel sorry for referees because their every decision is scrutinised and analysed so minutely that they must be frightened to be spontaneous. I fear they are weighed down with directives from above, told to clamp down on this and that, and it must be like trying to drive a car from the back seat. In my view, referees should stand up to their bosses, those who decide what constitutes a yellow card or even an offence, and tell them what it is like to officiate in the heat of a big match. The red card – a second yellow – for Arjen Robben of Chelsea for running into the crowd at

Sunderland in 2005/06 was ridiculous and typical of the way bureaucracy has replaced common sense and added to the huge burden referees must now work under.

The Welshman, Clive Thomas, was the worst of the major refs. He will be remembered for disallowing a Zico header by blowing for full-time half a second before Brazil netted against Sweden at a corner in the 1978 World Cup, having added only eight seconds extra; a monumental decision that only someone like him, out to make a name for himself, would have made. I don't think he had any time for anyone but Clive Thomas.

I am often asked if Manchester United get all the marginal decisions in their favour at Old Trafford. I'm bound to say I don't think so. Referees do not consciously give United any advantage and, in any case, it would be the same at Highbury for Arsenal and Anfield for Liverpool. Some referees may even act against Manchester United, as if to prove the lie to the accusations. I am sure Vic Callow, a top official in my time, had no axe to grind against us, but we at United will always remember how at Highbury in 1993/94, Callow sent off Eric Cantona in a clash with Nigel Winterburn.

Matches with Arsenal, then and now, were fierce affairs, and this was no different. A few days earlier Cantona had been sent off in a drawn match with Swindon and was already facing a ban. Cantona was in trouble again after he evaded a legitimate tackle from Winterburn but fell on the Arsenal left-back in trying to get out of the way. Arsenal made a terrible fuss, reacting furiously to a completely innocuous incident and, unbelievably, Callow showed Eric a red. Arsenal resented our success at the time and they got what they wanted as Eric was sent packing again.

But then matches against Arsenal and Liverpool were always huge for us at Manchester United. There was always an edge. In fact, oddly you might think, I had not realised until I stepped out of the game, just how big they were in the club calendar. Only after I had retired did I see by fan reaction, what it meant to beat those two clubs in particular. Defeating Manchester City was great, but there was only ever local pride at stake and City were never top of our must-win list.

Sir Alex was relaxed on the day of most of our matches but he was noticeably tenser when we were involved in the really big games. The boss was ultra-competitive and instilled in us the same desire for success. The feeling when we won those games was of massive elation, you could walk on air for days.

The routine for a home match day was much the same every game. Assuming it was a 3pm kick-off, admittedly rare these days, Sir Alex would come into the dressing room at 1.45pm and say what he required of us with a mixture of passion and calm authority. By the time he left us to our preparations ten minutes later, we all knew where we stood. He would then go to his office, chat to one or two close allies, or watch a bit of television, and not return until about ten minutes before kick-off. As we left to go out on to the pitch he shook our hands, patted us on the back and wished us good luck. The rest was up to us.

In my time, it was our coach Brian Kidd who spoke to us individually, soothing those who needed soothing, invigorating those who needed to be wound up. I think I was always just about the quietest man in our dressing room. That was my way. But there was a fire in the bellies of us all which I doubt exists in the same way now. With huge salaries at their disposal, the young lads appear not to have the same desire and I am not sure they could take the rollickings we took without collapsing.

Tea cups don't fly against the walls any more and I think even a man as passionate and caring as Sir Alex finds the modern-day player a different, mentally softer animal than those of a decade or more ago.

One man at United who was an exception to that observation was Wayne Rooney who went on, as we predicted he would, to become a dominant figure in English football. Whether or not Wayne became truly world-class, as he should have been, is another matter. His best years coincided with a decline in the quantity and quality of English players and the international success of 1966 and our own achievement in 1990 began to look like it was as good as it was ever going to get.

Chapter 14

Singapore's premier passions

Singapore, September 2012

MORE THAN six years after I wrote the majority of this book I am now based in Singapore and using my experience of English football and my background to bring some expertise to television coverage of the Premiership in these steamy Far Eastern islands.

Nicky and the boys love the lifestyle and there is plenty of work for me, so it has all panned out well so far. But it wasn't always like that. Writing this book raised my profile after some lean years following my retirement from football, which had been the only job I knew anything about. It got me a newspaper column in England, some commentary and punditry work with 5Live, BBC London, Capital Gold, worldwide radio for IMG and co-commentating for Setanta when they covered the Conference National for a year or two.

Oddly, my knowledge of the non-league scene through my days with Chelmsford and Welling rather than playing for England and Manchester United probably helped me get that particular role. But then things started to go a little sour. Setanta ran out of money, lost the Conference National coverage and the competition for the sort of jobs I was doing among ex-professionals was making it hard for me to get regular work. I was at a crossroads.

At a dinner at Doncaster, of all places, where I was meeting my old pal Ian Snodin, I spoke to a former Rovers apprentice who told me of opportunities in Australia and New Zealand where he wanted me to run a soccer school. On 28th August 2009 we left for Darwin in the Northern Territories on tourist visas and quickly came to enjoy the Aussie way of life and the sunshine.

But life didn't go smoothly. I fell out with the guy who had suggested I go out there – I don't want to name him – and he got his revenge by telling the immigration department that I had been working illegally. I had indeed flown down to Sydney to do some punditry for Fox (Australia's equivalent of Sky TV) with Robbie Slater, formerly of Blackburn and Southampton, and Mark Bosnich, who had played for Manchester United and Aston Villa. But that was for expenses only because I knew I was not allowed to work.

At the time I was also involved with the Football Federation of the Northern Territories who were extremely kind to me. They were keen for me to work for them and sponsored me for permanent residence, which would have enabled me to live and work in Australia, and the chief minister for the whole vast, thinly-populated region was going to endorse my application. But the immigration people, believing I was moonlighting, wouldn't let me rest, grilling me mercilessly for four hours based on malicious information incorrectly passed on, and on 6th January 2010 I had to leave Australia for a time without my family, heading for Singapore to do some work for ESPN.

All the while a generous Dutch-Australian named John Kop was fighting my corner even after my family had joined me in Singapore. Eventually in February 2010 I got the much-coveted PR, as it's known, but much as I enjoyed working for the FFNT, it was hard work convincing the locals in an area three times the size of Britain that football was the world's sport.

There was no more work for Fox so we headed back to Singapore, looking to get established. Simon Cook, a Singapore-based entrepreneur originally from Hull, helped smooth my path on permanent arrival in 2010, as did Dave and Jacinta Rowe, and we felt instantly at home. ESPN television promised me nothing but through them I got an employment pass and a Foreign Identification Number under the classification of "football consultant and media" because it is hard to get into Singapore even when there are some 800,000 foreign nationals in a total population of more than five million.

As it happened I soon got plenty of work in the media, talking about the Premiership and internationals for ESPN and then with Sing Tel who show English matches on TV here. I also got involved with Manchester United's business partners in Asia, wrote a ghosted column for Singapore's *The New Paper* and a Premiership blog for Yahoo. I play in the Masters tournament for Manchester United with players such as Bryan Robson, Andy Cole, Viv Anderson and Clayton Blackmore across Malaysia, Indonesia and Brunei and am a partner, dare it be said, in Arsenal's coaching franchise with JSSL Arsenal with two international schools and a third pending.

I carried out some punditry during Euro 2012 for Astro Supersport TV in Kuala Lumpur with more promised in the future and have been lined up to act as a mentor for a social project in Chomburi, outside Bangkok. All this has come about in two hectic years.

We live near the Malaysian border almost in the jungle, Nicky is now working for a fashion business and the boys, Jake and Max, attend British schools here, to which they have quickly adjusted. It's odd getting out of bed in the middle of the night to go to the studios to commentate on matches taking place several hours behind in England, but I am used to it now and there is no rush to return to England. Singapore is wealthy and I am also used to seeing the roads jammed with Ferraris and Lamborghinis. We are coming to terms with the heavy, tropical rain, the lightning and thunder and I think we have done better here than we could ever have expected when on a whim we uprooted in 2008.

My job is very much connected with the state and health of football back in England and I'm not sure the patient is especially well. I don't gain any pleasure from saying so and I don't want to bite the hand that has been feeding me but I wonder if England will ever win a major tournament again. The talk is still of 1966 and even of 1990 when I was in the team which got through to the semi-finals of the World Cup. For this the Football Association must take some responsibility and show a bit of leadership in restoring the country to its former eminence. In terms of footballing countries the plain fact is that we are no longer in the top division. When did England last beat one of the big nations when it matters? And do the FA accept that England is no longer a top-notch football power?

The Premiership gives a false impression of English football because great though it is to watch and commentate upon, it is stuffed full of foreign players, some of whom are far better than others. The FA has to take a step backwards to go forwards, but I'm not sure they realise this or want to do anything about it. The Premiership is killing young British players because not enough of them get opportunities to play in it.

Don't get me wrong, the Premiership is a great product with a worldwide audience numbered in billions, as well I know from the level of interest in Singapore. But it is harming the home products, like a car running over kids. Would Ryan Giggs, for instance, get a chance to make his debut at 17 nowadays? I doubt it. Our top teenagers should be training with the best foreign imported players instead of being shunted out on loan to clubs in the lower leagues.

How nice it was to see Ryan Bertrand, for instance, get his belated chance with Chelsea in the Champions League final after going to half a dozen lower league clubs on loan. Too many like him become disillusioned at their lack of opportunities. If you play on loan for too long in the Championship or League 1, you become a Championship or League 1 player. Too much talent is therefore being stifled and wasted.

The FA should be using the Under-21s as a bridging process because the truth of the matter is that we are running out of quality players. When I think back to my time, I remember the players who couldn't get into the England team because the competition was so fierce. Tony Adams couldn't get into our squad in 1990, while really good players like Steve Bull and Steve McMahon played so little. We've always been spoiled for goalkeepers but now there is Joe Hart and, er, Joe Hart. There is no international-calibre left-back now that Ashley Cole is coming towards the end and while I recognise Scott Parker is an industrious, highly effective domestic player, he's not international class.

Roy Hodgson must have been delighted to have got the manager's job until he sat down and sifted through the names of the players he had available to him at Euro 2012 and realised how few of them would frighten the likes of Italy and Germany. Try naming 23 players. They talk of the "golden" generation of Frank Lampard, Steven Gerrard, Rio Ferdinand, Cole and David Beckham but no way, for example, was Lampard ever a complete midfield player in the way, say, Steve McMahon was. All he does is shoot. And they have won nothing for England or even got close to it, so they are hardly "golden".

I'm being told Jack Wilshere is one player who might come through and head a new generation but first he needs to be playing regularly for Arsenal, which has not been the case. And I'm fed up with Theo Walcott. He is beyond the "promising" stage but if you want raw pace, why not sign

Usain Bolt? As for Alex Oxlade-Chamberlain, my old boss Fergie would never have allowed him to play for England until he felt he was ready, mentally and physically. He is still, in my opinion, a long way short of being properly prepared. The obvious answer is for the FA to impose a foreign quota. But do they have the guts to do it? I doubt it. Managers are scared of using young English players because a defeat, even a single setback, could be costly in terms of prize money. Foreign owner egos are also getting in the way of progress.

What I do like is that results in the Premiership are slightly less predictable than they used to be. I hated the way Neil Warnock, Gary Megson and Mick McCarthy rested their top players for games against the big clubs on the basis they would probably lose anyway. Now so-called lesser clubs are much more prepared to attack, home and away.

In the season which finished just before I sat down to write this epilogue, Wigan and Blackburn each beat Manchester United and in effect cost them the title and I know as a player how I wanted to play at all the big grounds and show what I could do. To be deprived by cautious management was unacceptable and now, thankfully, it's all a lot more optimistic and aggressive.

As I write, Sir Alex retains an immense position of power at Manchester United and within the game generally. Fergie understands players, when to get rid of them, when to remove them from doing damage in the dressing room and he seems to be no less influential or involved than when he first arrived at Old Trafford from Aberdeen. He wakes up every morning hungry for success as much as he did 25 years ago.

I love watching Arsenal but all these years on they still miss David Seaman and a proper centre-half or two while Chelsea have much to do, despite their Champions League achievement, to reclaim their credibility and get back to their fans. They need to be seen to be managed.

Am I envious of the wages? I'm bound to say I was born ten or 20 years too soon but I don't begrudge modern players their wealth. However I do believe that too many average players have become millionaires and lost their ambition. Are they providing quality in keeping with their wage packets? I'm not so sure. If they were actors at a theatre, the audience would want its money back far too often.

As for the diving phenomenon which has afflicted English football in recent years, I have to register my disappointment that it continues to bedevil our game. We used to blame foreign players for falling over and feigning injury but ours are just as guilty now. I can't understand why so many modern players throw themselves to the floor and why is it when a player has his shirt pulled he falls forwards? Just an observation, but the honesty and humour seems to have gone, which I regard as a great shame, as have the personalities. If a player is tripped he wants a fight. I can never understand that, but these may be considered to be the gripes of a middle-aged ex-player and I hope that you can see through them to realise that I love the game and want it to flourish. I want England to win another World Cup. Is that too much to ask?

Racism is now an issue in football but, believe me, it has always been there, as passages of this book have indicated. When I was insulted as Patrice Evra and Anton Ferdinand appear to have been I would speak to the black players on the other side, a quiet word to ask if they were happy with what a team-mate of theirs was saying to me. I like to think it had an effect.

In those days we were perhaps a little more thick-skinned about what was said on a pitch. I was unhappy to see the John Terry case go to a court of law. In my view it should never have got that far but the FA bottled it, as they have done with so many important matters. As soon as the accusation against Terry was made public, witnessed by millions on television, the FA should have dealt with it immediately. It was the same too with Luis Suarez. I'm convinced, incidentally, that the well-meaning support of Suarez by his manager got Kenny Dalglish the sack.

One remedy would be to get rid of the pre-match handshakes. I find them ridiculous, unnecessary and pointless. Save the handshakes for the proper time at the end of a match. But they came about as the result of a Fifa directive, designed to foster good relations, and the FA would need to stand up for itself and say to them: "Not in England".

Talking of the Terry case, I found it embarrassing that the court case was delayed until after Euro 2012 but, as I say, it might all have been settled had the FA acted decisively from the start, rather than let it fester. I think too that Fabio Capello knew what he was doing in resigning over the Terry captaincy issue. He could see the England cupboard was bare and got out of the way, his reputation untarnished by failure. Were the FA conned here? I think so.

So much for the present state of the game. My main task was to look back and now I must choose a best 11 from those I played with and against. There are so many contenders, few certainties and many near misses. My selection should have been based on a 4-4-2 system which was prevalent in my playing days and is still favoured in England, though not so much abroad. Players in England have always liked to be told what to do and I speak as an ex-player and as an ex-manager. They love to know their exact job.

I just wish there were more free spirits, like Gascoigne at his best, in helping me with my choices. I have cheated slightly in going for a 4-4-1-1 system to accommodate one special talent. In goal it was easier to choose between Peter Schmeichel and David Seaman than I thought it would be and there were no other serious contenders. I have gone for Schmeichel on the basis that he was very different from any keeper I knew. Seaman was outstanding in an orthodox, conventional way, marking lines in his area so that he always knew where he was. Peter Shilton was the same, everything had to be in its place. Big Schmeichel would never have written a book on how to keep goal because he was instinctive and unusual, his philosophy based on his experience as a handball player in Denmark.

Ron Springett kept goal for England in 33 internationals up to 1966 and was a member of the World Cup-winning squad. I remember, as a boy, the coaching manual he produced. Peter would never have featured in it as a role model for kids. Peter did everything his way and is definitely my number one.

There was no better full-back than Denis Irwin. He could play on either flank with consistency and conviction. He was as happy on his left as he was on his right. Not many can do that, certainly I couldn't. I liked the way he could open up his left side so that he appeared to be naturally left-footed, a skill not readily appreciated except by those who have tried and failed.

Lee Dixon is now an accomplished pundit and although I didn't play with him I admired the way he responded to Arsene Wenger's continental thinking and as a result gained an extra dimension. David Bardsley was a dressing room prankster at Queens Park Rangers but a lack of confidence stopped him gaining any more than two caps. He had the talent for more. Gary Stevens was a good all-rounder and fantastically fit. When England carried out bleep tests, Gary would keep us waiting because he could reach level 16 and needed to be told to stop.

As for left-back, my choice is Stuart Pearce. Pearce was by far the best left-back of his era although Kenny Sansom was a favourite of mine. I also played with the under-rated Mark Dennis and it was a bit of a travesty that his international career was limited to three Under-21 caps. Mark had a superb left foot and it was only when I played alongside him that I realised just how good he was. He trained the way he played, with fierce determination. I used to jump out of the way of tackles in training, but not Mark. His problem was a poor disciplinary record but I found him to be an intelligent footballer and misunderstood.

My central defenders should be Steve Bruce and Gary Pallister but there was plenty of competition. Pallister had that extra pace, which lifted him clear of contemporaries but there would not have been much in it if ever he raced Des Walker. Considering he was the smaller, Bruce won more headers than Pallister but Pally never got the credit he deserved for what he could do on the ball. Opponents thought Bruce and Pallister struggled with the ball at their feet, but they were rarely exposed.

Terry Butcher was an inspiration, Des Walker was undone by the back-pass rule change while the late Alan McDonald was a top-class player who might have spent too long at QPR. Big blond Roger Brown, now also dead, would be flattered to find himself mentioned in such company but he was a tremendous player at Fulham but who came into the game a little too late. Terry Fenwick was sly, cute, streetwise, but a great organiser. Mark Wright had pace, bravery and strength in the air and I am sure Tony Gale would have played for England had his heading matched his terrific passing and tackling.

Ultimately though it was a toss-up between Pallister and the great Tony Adams to partner Bruce and although I feel Pallister would have better complemented Bruce, I find it hard to look beyond Adams.

Andrei Kanchelskis had such strong legs he could keep a medicine ball in the air with the same ease and control as any other player might have done with a football. It was his party piece and it drove Fergie mad, but he forgave him because he was a special player and normal rules did not apply. Kanchelskis lived life in the way he played, at great pace. He picked up speeding tickets as regularly as he skipped past full-backs and nothing bothered him for long. The Ukrainian never mastered English but we had an understanding down the right wing which transcended any language. He bombed forward, I stayed back and we knew each other's strengths and weaknesses. His great asset, standing behind him, was in taking opponents away from me and our fans loved him for the way he also contributed spectacular goals.

Chris Waddle was a fabulous player on the right side of midfield although he was essentially left-footed while I also came to appreciate Ray Houghton's less flamboyant style when he arrived at Fulham. Houghton seemed odd to me when I was an apprentice, supposedly Scottish yet with a Cockney accent and a desire to play for the Republic of Ireland, which he did. He got better and better, blossoming at Oxford and flowering at Liverpool where his intelligent passing and eye-catching volleys earned him proper recognition. My choice is Waddle because of his greater passing range.

On the left side of midfield there was only one serious candidate in Ryan Giggs. He came to our attention as a 16-year-old and 20 or so years later he was still playing in the Olympics, an absolute once-in-a-generation phenomenon. I always thought Lee Sharpe had as much natural talent when he came to us from Torquay and was an exceptional crosser but he had a sort of maverick mentality which diverted his attention too often elsewhere. Lee will go down as an unfulfilled talent, but he was different. While the rest of us headed for resorts for our holidays, Lee got out his rucksack and headed to obscure places unknown to the rest of us.

Andy Sinton, now a non-league manager, got 12 England caps and was a great player for QPR. He was my room-mate and his quick feet could give us an early advantage in any move.

My two central midfielders are Gascoigne and Roy Keane. I think Gazza should have joined Manchester United so that he could have got the best from his extraordinary ability because he would have been subjected to greater discipline and made us a better team. I wonder if his fellow Geordie Waddle influenced him to join Spurs instead.

Roy Keane was an incredible midfield force and although Paul Ince ran him close, Roy was more versatile and more likely to score. None of us minded Ince calling himself "the Guv'nor". His Mercedes bore the number plate L8 GUV and it boosted his ego without interfering with ours.

I was fortunate to play alongside Bryan Robson for England and Manchester United and Peter Reid made me think more about the game when he came to QPR. Ray Wilkins was a man of integrity, a gentleman on and off the pitch. He should have been a bank manager, such was his demeanour. Ray was vilified for his square and back passing but he was ahead of his time in that he never liked to waste a ball.

Eric Cantona is the reason for my 4-4-1-1 system, playing him just behind Mark Hughes, the sole forward in my team. Eric was not quite a midfield player and not quite a forward but Teddy Sheringham was the only player subsequently able to score and make goals. Jurgen Klinsmann transformed Sheringham from a conventional centre forward and the two of us were rare creatures at Manchester United because Fergie did not like Londoners. In fact I think it fair to say he hated them and much enjoyed beating London clubs. He thought Londoners soft, prone to moaning and not as committed as those from elsewhere. In my time Ince was the only other major player from the capital until David Beckham came along. I can only imagine David must have personified all Fergie's fears about Londoners rolled into one although he was of course an outstanding player and became a world-famous personality.

"Sparky" Hughes was a problem to play against because of his great strength. In a physical battle, which he relished, there was only ever going to be one winner when I played against him. I was grateful only to ever play against him twice a year, although he had no great pace and didn't like chasing. My only hope was to nick the ball off him, but as he shielded it so well, that was no easy task. I preferred playing with him because you could give him the ball in any position and nine times out of ten he would retain it under any pressure. Hughes left United because he did not fancy being a squad player, although the manager wanted to retain him, but he was well regarded subsequently at Chelsea, Everton and Southampton.

Gary Lineker's international goal tally puts him second only to Bobby Charlton but I'm not sure he was as complete a player as Hughes while there were three other top-class players whom I was lucky enough to call team-mates. Trevor Francis was not the bravest and would never play through the pain barrier but when he was 100 per cent, he was one of the best strikers I ever saw. His greatest asset was his lightning change of pace and the hat-trick he got at Villa for QPR was one of the best of my career. Brian McClair loved Manchester United, never hid from the flak and was a good all-rounder. Andy Cole became a better player for joining Manchester United where we made him learn to play with his back to goal and add more to his game than be the pure goal-scorer of his Newcastle days. Replacing Hughes, as he did, was a thankless task but he accomplished it eventually and at his peak should have won many more caps. Glenn Hoddle, the England coach at the time, made the comment that Andy was prone to missing too many chances and one goal in 15 appearances over seven years means he was probably right.

So my final line-up is Schmeichel; Irwin, Bruce, Adams, Pearce; Waddle, Gascoigne, Keane, Giggs; Cantona; Hughes.

The one player I would have loved to have played alongside is Franco Baresi of AC Milan. I loved watching the Milan defence of the 1980s. As a defender I relished the way they squeezed high up the pitch, making forwards think and work hard for any hint of an opening. Baresi never allowed his direct opponent the chance to rest or settle. I would have liked to have played directly against John Barnes, just to test myself. I know he would not have beaten me for pace at best. It was odd that we never got the chance to confront each other.

My favourite and least favourite ground? I loved playing at Goodison Park. There was always an unbelievable atmosphere, a real footballing environment in a traditional, old-style stadium. A great place. The one I disliked most was Selhurst Park. When I was there with Fulham and QPR, I found it to be lifeless and dull because the terraces never seemed to be full. It was better when I went back with Manchester United when there were more people inside. I don't think Eric Cantona liked Selhurst Park much either.

Size does matter, take my word for it. I hope my story has given some encouragement to those who, like me, never got much beyond 5ft 7ins in a game more and more populated by giants. I can honestly say being small bothered other people more than it bothered me. If it affected me in any way it made me more determined to get the better of players far bigger and more often than not I succeeded, otherwise I would not have played at the level I did.

To have played for England while lacking height, I needed at least one major, major asset and I had two, my pace and my ability to jump. They carried me through 16 years of football, so that acquiring skills like positioning came with experience. My shortage of inches never concerned the best manager of modern times. Sir Alex brought me to the biggest club in the country and told me to do what I was good at. For everything Sir Alex did for me, it was Ray Harford who saved me from football oblivion. When I was going through that lull, that long spell at Fulham when progress was retarded, he took me aside and told me a few home truths. He continued to do that even when my career took off. "The time I'm not interested," he said, "is the time I don't care."

Did I get the best out of myself as a player? No. I always think there is more I could have done, more I could have achieved. I didn't work hard enough to get fit when I was injured and there is more I could have done to look after my body. The temptation in your 20s is to believe you can go on for ever. I should have played more for England although I feel I did myself justice when I wore the three lions.

I think I lacked a certain sense of self-confidence which I saw in others, a natural gift, and wished I had been more assertive. I believe I am now in footballing retirement but I was less so then. I stood up for myself but I never had that swagger which Ince, Robson and Keane had among my contemporaries. I think I was liked. I was never a bully, nor was I bullied. I like to think also that I did black people a service by showing that it was possible to succeed in football in England as one of the first to play in internationals, and now there are plenty who have followed.

If there was a word to describe me as a player it was "competitive". I had to be. Playing for Manchester United gave me a presence, a responsibility and it made me feel special. I regret the way I slid out of the game but I'm over it now and the love affair, even from here in Singapore, is back on. Sir Bobby Robson summed me up perfectly when he compared me to a fish and a rodent. I thank him for his unusual description because I think it fitted me perfectly. "Leaps like a salmon, tackles like a ferret."

Career statistics
– compiled by Jim Baldwin

Paul Andrew Parker
Birthplace: West Ham
Date of birth: 4th April 1964

	League		Lge Cup		FA Cup		Europe		Other	
	A	*G*	*A*	*G*	*A*	*G*	*A*	*G*	*A*	*G*
Fulham										
80/81	1	0	0	0	0	0	0	0	0	0
81/82	2+3	0	0	0	0	0	0	0	0	0
82/83	6+11	0	2	0	3	0	0	0	0	0
83/84	34	0	4	0	2	0	0	0	0	0
84/85	36	0	3	0	1	0	0	0	0	0
85/86	30	0	3	0	1	0	0	0	1	0
86/87	31	2	4	1	4	0	0	0	1	0
QPR										
87/88	40	0	3	0	4	0	0	0	1	0
88/89	36	0	6	0	3	0	0	0	3	0
89/90	32	0	2	0	9	0	0	0	0	0
90/91	13+4	1	3	0	0	0	0	0	1	0
Manchester United										
91/92	24+2	0	6	0	3	0	2	0	0	0
92/93	31	1	2	0	3	0	0+1	0	0	0
93/94	39+1	0	6	0	7	0	3	0	1	0
94/95	1+1	0	0	0	0	0	2+1	0	0	0
95/96	5+1	0	1	0	1+1	1	0+1	0	0	0
Derby County										
96/97	4	0	2	0	0	0	0	0	0	0

	League		Lge Cup		FA Cup		Europe		Other	
	A	G	A	G	A	G	A	G	A	G
Sheffield United										
96/97	7+3	0	0	0	0	0	0	0	0	0
Fulham										
96/97	3	0	0	0	0	0	0	0	0	0
Chelsea										
96/97	1+3	0	0	0	0	0	0	0	0	0
Total	376+29	4	47	1	41+1	1	7+3	0	8	0

SUMMARY

	League		Lge Cup		FA Cup		Europe		Other	
Fulham	143+14	2	16	1	11	0	0	0	2	0
QPR	121+4	1	14	0	16	0	0	0	5	0
Manchester United	100+5	1	15	0	14+1	1	7+3	0	1	0
Derby County	4	0	2	0	0	0	0	0	0	0
Sheffield United	7+3	0	0	0	0	0	0	0	0	0
Chelsea	1+3	0	0	0	0	0	0	0	0	0

Notes:
A = appearances, denoting starts + appearances as a substitute.
The Europe column includes European Cup Winners' Cup (1991/92), Uefa Cup (1992/93 and 1995/96), European Cup (1993/94) and Champions League (1994/95).
Other includes Full Members Cup (1985/86), Freight Rover Trophy (1986/87), Simod Cup (1987/88 and 1988/89), Mercantile Credit Centenary Trophy (1988/89) and Charity Shield (1993/94).

GOALS

Fulham v Aldershot at Craven Cottage on 3rd September 1986 (League Cup first round second leg, won 2-0).

Fulham v Chester City at Sealand Road on 6th September 1986 (drew 2-2).

Fulham v Chesterfield at Craven Cottage on 11th April 1987 (won 3-1).

QPR v Luton Town at Loftus Road on 15th September 1990 (won 6-1).

Manchester United v Tottenham Hotspur at Old Trafford on 9th January 1993 (won 4-1).

Manchester United v Reading at Elm Park on 27th January 1996 (FA Cup fourth round, won 3-0).

CLUB HONOURS (All with Manchester United)

Rumbelows Football League Cup 1992
Premiership 1992/93 and 1993/94
Charity Shield 1993
FA Cup 1994

CAREER MILESTONES

100th league appearance: For Fulham v Wimbledon at Plough Lane on 12th October 1985.

200th league appearance: For QPR v Millwall at The Den on 1st October 1988.

300th league appearance: For Manchester United v Crystal Palace at Old Trafford on 22nd February 1992.

400th league appearance: For Fulham v Cardiff City at Craven Cottage on 31st January 1997.

FIRST AND LAST LEAGUE APPEARANCES

Fulham: Debut v Reading at Craven Cottage on 25th April 1981; last appearance v Cardiff City at Craven Cottage on 31st January 1997.

QPR: Debut v West Ham United at Upton Park on 15th August 1987; last appearance v Everton at Loftus Road on 11th May 1991.

Manchester United: Debut v Notts County at Old Trafford on 17th August 1991; last appearance v Tottenham Hotspur at White Hart Lane on 1st January 1996.

Derby County: Debut v Leeds United at the Baseball Ground on 17th August 1996; last appearance v Sheffield Wednesday at Hillsborough on 21st September 1996.

Sheffield United: Debut v Port Vale at Vale Park on 16th November 1996; last appearance v Bradford City at Valley Parade on 26th December 1996.

Chelsea: Debut v Sunderland at Stamford Bridge on 16th March 1997; last appearance v Arsenal at Stamford Bridge on 5th April 1997.

Consecutive league appearances: 64 for Queens Park Rangers, from 15th August 1987 to 11th February 1989.

Paul Parker did not miss a league game during the 1987/88 season for QPR and was the only Rangers player to achieve this feat during the season.

MISCELLANEOUS

Paul played in all four levels of English professional football during his career, plus every round of the League Cup and FA Cup ("proper stages", i.e post-qualifying rounds).

Of his 405 league appearances, 238 (59%) were in the top flight (Premiership 87, First Division prior to 1992/93 151); 127 (31%) in First Division (post-1992/93) and Second Division (pre-1992/93); 37 (9%) in Second Division (post-1992/93) and Third Division (pre-1992/93); 3 (1%) in Third Division (post-1992/93).

INTERNATIONAL HONOURS
England Youth
Appearances: 1+2

Goals: 0

Substitute v Sweden at Pazin on 5th September 1981 (international tournament in Yugoslavia).

Substitute v Yugoslavia at Pula on 10th September 1981 (international tournament final in Yugoslavia).